Adopted and Blessed

Words from my heart

SHARLA YNOSTROSA

ISBN 978-1-63525-663-5 (Paperback)
ISBN 978-1-63525-665-9 (Hard Cover)
ISBN 978-1-63525-664-2 (Digital)

Christian Faith Publishing, Inc.
296 Chestnut Street
Meadville, PA 16335
www.christianfaithpublishing.com

Printed in the United States of America

My heart is so full I have so much to say
It is gorgeous outside, the start of a beautiful new day.
This morning, I woke with a pain in my heart
Knowing my mission, just not sure where to start!

God has opened my eyes and has touched my heart.
To save the unborn, I must do my part.

What should I do? What do I say?
I ask the Lord as I pray and pray.
He fills my head with words to say,
So I write, and I write each and every day.

I cry out to Him to show me the way.
How do I make a difference today?
I just don't understand why it's so hard to see,
The horrible death that abortion brings.
What must I do? What must I say?
So I write, and I write each and every day.

I send letters to the paper. I write posts for my blog.
I put pictures on Facebook, and pray for new laws.
I weep for the babies, their innocent lives lost.

What am I missing? Am I not doing enough?
Please, God, help me. Please show me the way.
How can I make a difference today?

Then my heart begins to ache
I know I must speak up!
I know God is telling me, "Don't you dare give up!"
Keep going. Keep writing. Don't you see?
What you do makes a difference. You are listening to me!

It matters to God! It matters to Him!
I will write, and I will post, and I will write again.
I won't give up. I will be their voice!
I will fight for the unborn, because they are babies, not a choice!

Precious little babies in your mother's womb,
You are not a choice. You are a blessing, a gift from God.
I will speak up for you, and I will fight for your life.
I will write letters and posts and pray.
I will speak up for you each and every day!

Starting a Blog: Sharing My Stories

Saturday, March 22, 2014

Hello out there! My name is Sharla, and I was adopted at birth. I started this blog to help promote adoption as a life option. I was adopted from Ft. Worth, TX, fifty years ago. I was blessed with wonderful parents and a protective older brother. I've been happily married for almost thirty-one years now, and my husband, Jim, is an amazing man. When we got married, I was blessed with a six-year-old stepson, whom I love as my own. My husband and I were then blessed with two more children, a son and a daughter. We have eight grandchildren, six girls and two boys, all between the ages of nine months and eight years old!

This blog is going to be positive, full of life, and informational. I'm excited to get started. I will post links to pro-life websites, talk about good books, and share stories about my crazy, wonderful life!

2013 Summer Memories with Our Grandchildren

07/14/2013

Day Two

Sunday, March 23, 2014

Hello out there! This is my second post. I'm just learning about all this tech stuff, so hang in there for me (I'm not even on Facebook).

To the birth mothers out there who have chosen or are thinking about choosing adoption for their babies, thank you. Placing your baby up for adoption is a giving, selfless act. I pray that you will be given all the loving and emotional support you need to do this. I was adopted when I was three days old, and I will always be thankful that my birth mother gave me life by choosing adoption.

The Gladney Home in Ft. Worth, TX, helps young women who want/need to put their baby up for adoption. I'll post a link to their website later tonight.

I've got to go now. My husband is reminding me that it is time to leave for Mass.

I Have to Do Something

Thursday, March 27, 2014

Hello out there! I hope you are having a great day! It's beautiful here in San Angelo. Hopefully, we will be blessed with rain soon. I'm not sure how often I should attach a post. I really don't know much about blogs at all. So you're probably thinking, "Then why did you start one?"

If you read my previous posts, you'll notice the links I attached to the letters I had published in the newspaper. When I feel really strong about something, the words just come to me. After my daughter read the letter I had written in July 2013, she told me that if I really wanted to get my message out there that I would have to use the social networking sites. I started saying that I was going to start a blog, and that made everyone laugh because I don't even have a Facebook page. I have an older cell phone, and it does not have a texting keyboard, so it takes me forever to reply to a text, unless my response is okay, yes, no, etc. After my letter in January was published, my husband, kids, and some really close friends encouraged me to do more to get my pro-life message out there. That's where this blog comes in. I'm just telling my story, trying to promote adoption as the life option, as the life choice.

I wish I could explain how heavy the pro-life issue weighs on my heart, at least with this blog. Even though I'm totally out of my element, I know I'm trying to do something. In my Catholic daily meditations book *The Word among Us*, the response today is from Psalm 95, "If today you hear his voice, harden not your hearts."

On a lighter note, the Catholic radio station in San Angelo and the surrounding areas is 91.5, and it is a really informative station. If you aren't Catholic and have questions, the apologetics are on from 5:00 p.m. to 7:00 p.m. central time, and they answer all kinds of questions. There is great programming all throughout the day. My favorite is when they sing the Divine Mercy Chaplet at 3:00 p.m.

I'll close this post with a verse that always makes me think of the blessings of adoption, "He gives the childless woman a family, making her a happy mother. Praise the Lord!" (Psalm 113:9).

The Harsh Reality

Thursday, April 24, 2014

Do you ever have a moment when something really grabs your heart? You know, all of a sudden, you think of something that you just have to talk about? You just need someone to understand what you are trying to say? Well, this is it for me. This is my moment. I was scrolling past the pictures I've posted on my blog, and I came to the picture of the Pro-Life Rams hammering the crosses into the ground at ASU to display the Cemetery of the Innocents, and all of a sudden, I realized that babies who are aborted aren't even buried. They are not even buried! These innocent babies are not even buried! The remains of aborted babies are picked up by a medical waste truck, to be thrown away like garbage. I know this is not something anyone wants to hear. It's not something I even want to think about, but it is the truth, and that is why we have to stop abortion. We have to! A baby is a gift from God. A baby is not medical waste. Oh my gosh, why? How can we let this happen?

I know that most of you who read my blog feel like I do, and I'm thankful for all your encouragement and support. I know that many of you work hard for the pro-life movement, stand up for the pro-life movement, but if there is someone reading this blog who wants to do something but doesn't know what to do or where to start, here are some suggestions. Please pray for an end to abortion. Vote for an end to abortion. Speak up about the ugly truth of abortion. Buy a pro-life bumper sticker. Do something. Anything is better than nothing.

That is why I started this blog. I pray that this blog will help someone make a life choice. I pray that someone who reads this blog will guide someone else to make a life choice. I don't know if this blog will ever help anyone. I want it to. I pray it does, but at least I know I'm trying to do something. I will not give up. I will not be silent.

Please, God, open our eyes. Open our ears. Touch our hearts. Give us the strength, guidance, and discernment to stop abortion. In Jesus's holy name I pray, amen.

"Our battle is not against human forces but against the principalities and powers, the rulers of this world of darkness, the evil spirits in regions above" (Ephesians 6:12).

Saturday, May 3, 2014

Today is a very special day for our family. Two of my grandchildren will receive their first Holy Communion tonight. My daughter and son also received their first Holy Communion at Sacred Heart many years ago, and to see his son and her daughter receive Communion for the first time, at the same church, will truly be a blessing for us all! They are so excited, and we can't wait for Mass!

Have a wonderful, blessed weekend! Ours will be busy, but a joyful, great kind of busy!

Then taking a cup he offered a blessing in thanks and said;

> "Take this and divide it among you; I tell you, from now on I will not drink of the fruit of the vine until the coming of the reign of God."

Then, taking the bread and giving thanks, he broke it and gave it to them, saying;

> "This is my body to be given for you. Do this as a remembrance of me." He did the same with the cup after eating, saying as he did so: "This cup is the new covenant in my blood, which will be shed for you. (Luke 22:17–20)

Our Family Foundation
Our Faith

Tuesday, May 27, 2014

Good morning out there! We have been blessed with so much rain the last couple of days! The lake levels are way up, and the ground is saturated. Hooray! Thank You, Jesus!

My husband and I will be married thirty-one years next week! I think about all the things that have changed during our marriage: different jobs, different homes, all the different stages of our children's lives, and now we have eight amazing grandchildren, gifts from God! So many blessings, so much love, and I am so thankful!

The one thing that has stayed the same all these years is our parish home, Sacred Heart Cathedral. This is where we raised our children. This is where we grew as a family. Many wonderful memories are from when we were at Mass. Not only did we celebrate the joy of baptisms, first Communions, confirmations, and weddings, we also mourned the death of many loved ones at funeral Masses.

We didn't, and don't, just attend Mass. We were and are involved. My children became altar servers just as soon as they could. My husband has been an usher for years, and I have been honored to serve as a lector, a commentator, and humbled to serve as a Eucharistic minister. Many times over the years, I would be standing at the front of the cathedral waiting to lector, and Jim would be standing at the back where the ushers are, but I could always spot him in an instant.

I remember one time he was in the balcony and I looked up and saw him. My heart stopped for just a second, and I just thought how blessed I was to be married to such a wonderful man. Even though we rarely sit together, we are together. A wave across the church, a smile, a feeling—we are always together.

We have seen many children grow up at Sacred Heart—from babies to toddlers, then teens, then young adults. We have always enjoyed the holidays when many return home and attend Mass.

This past Sunday Evening in Mass, I was at the front, Jim was at the back, and young married couples with small children and babies on the way were everywhere. So much new life! My heart was so full. So many of these couples, I had known at least one of them since they were a small child, and now they have families of their own. Our children and grandchildren are at Mass with us most times, at Sacred Heart, our home.

Today, I pray that each of you will be blessed with a home like ours and that no matter where you sit or stand, you will always be together.

> You are God's chosen race, his saints; he loves you, and you should be clothed in sincere compassion, in kindness and humility, gentleness and patience.

> Bear with one another; forgive each other as soon as a quarrel begins. The Lord has forgiven you; now you must do the same. Over all these clothes, to keep them together and complete them, put on love.

> And may the peace of Christ reign in your hearts, because it is for this that you were

called together as parts of one body. Always be thankful.

Let the message of Christ, in all its richness, find a home with you. Teach each other, and advise each other, in all wisdom. With gratitude in your hearts sing psalms and hymns and inspired songs to God; and never say or do anything except in the name of the Lord Jesus, giving thanks to God the Father through him. (Colossians 3:12–17)

A Wedding Is a Day,
A Marriage Is a Lifetime

Wednesday, June 4, 2014

Hello out there! My husband and I have been married for thirty-one years today! I think that every year should be a celebration! Life is such a gift, and I don't ever want to take it for granted. We should never take our spouses for granted either. I really believe in not sweating the small stuff. A wedding is a day; a marriage is a lifetime. A good, healthy, happy, and loving marriage takes work. I am very blessed, very thankful, and I love being a wife, mother, and grandmother. I listen to the Catholic Radio Station, Guadalupe Radio Network 91.5 FM, when I am running all my errands. (I always wanted to be a DJ in my spare time!) This morning, they told us about a website for married couples. It is Foryourmarriage.org

I looked up the site and was thrilled with all the different types of information they have for engaged couples and married couples. This is a Catholic marriage website, but I think it would be great for everyone!

They have a daily marriage tip, scriptures, different family perspectives, and all kinds of great, loving, prayerful advice. I'm going to end my blog today with the marriage tip they had for May 29, 2014, and a scripture they had for another day.

"What lifts up your spirit? Is it a funny story, a good meal, a hug, a compliment? Lift up each other today!" (I think that is great advice. We should always try to lift up our spouse, not bring them down.)

"All these devoted themselves with one accord to prayer" (Acts 1:14). Pray with each other and for each other. Pray with your children. Let prayer be a top priority in your family.

I thought of something else I wanted to add. Laugh, sing, and dance. I can't tell you how many times I've gone out to check on Jim when he's working in the shop (he always has the radio on, listening to a country western station), and we will two-step around the welding machine and other assorted equipment! Live life with lots of joy in your heart, and love will bloom all around.

Bye for now.

Sharla

Tuesday, June 17, 2014

Good morning out there! You will not believe what I was doing about thirty minutes ago! I looked out my kitchen window, and there in my front yard were fifteen of my six- to eight-week-old chickens running around. By the time I got outside, they were crossing the street. A truck was stopped waiting for them to cross. I waved kind of sheepishly and then darted out to the street as soon as he drove off! I was hollering, "Get back over here!" Although it came out more like "Git back over here" every now, and then my Texas twang really comes out. I'm sure this was one of those times! I mean, how do you call a chicken to come home? Anyway, of course, they thought I was going to feed them, so they all came running. I just hope none of my neighbors were filming this. If there is a crazy chicken chasing scene on Youtube later, more than likely it is of me and my chickens! Anyway, I told them to go back in the field where they belong, but they didn't. So I came back inside, grabbed my camera, and took pictures of them. Yes, I posted a picture of them in my front yard!

Have a great day! Bye for now.
Sharla

Live life with a song in your heart!

Thursday, June 19, 2014

Hello out there. My heart is sad today. I wish I knew what to say. I try to make people see, the gift of life a baby will be. Please, God, show me the way, so that I can make a difference today. As tears stream down my face, why does my heart ache this way? Please, God, give me the words. Please guide my hand as I write this verse. How do I make others see, the horrible death that abortion brings. Please give me strength. Please give me courage to fight this fight that curses the earth. Please, God, show me the way, that I can make a difference today.

Gifts from heaven, babies are, gifts from God above. Protect them, love them, sing songs of joy. New life, new life—how precious they are.

I write the way I feel. My emotions so very real. I'm praying for a way to help the unborn today. All babies are gifts and need our love. Their innocence, their dependence—they need us. I will speak up for them as long as I have voice because the ones I fight for are babies, and not a choice!

Bye for now.
Sharla

Saturday, June 21, 2014

Good morning out there! We have been blessed with more rain! It is a beautiful, cloudy, homemade "chicken soup" kind of day! I've got a big pot of chicken noodle soup simmering on the stove and a fresh pitcher of ice tea ready to drink! I'll heat up some buttered French bread, and lunch will be served!

I really enjoy writing posts for my blog; it is like a journal for me. Someday, my grandkids will grow up and have families of their own. I hope that they will read the archives from my blog, and not only remember how very much I love them, what gifts their lives are to me, but what I stand for, what I believe in. I hope it will help guide them along their life's pathway.

I read an article that was in Wednesday's newspaper. It was an article about Wendy Davis, her filibuster last year, and several pro-abortion groups celebrating the one year anniversary on June 25. I've been thinking and praying about my response to the article. So here it goes.

This was the headline: "Advocates Mark Filibuster Anniversary, Pro-Abortion Rights Groups Renew Efforts."

The following paragraph is why I knew I had to speak my mind: "This month, in a fundraising email, the Davis campaign let supporters have a chance to win a pair of pink running shoes like the ones Davis wore during her filibuster."

I feel like my best response is the letter I wrote to the newspaper that was published in the View Points Section in the San Angelo Standard Times Newspaper after her filibuster last summer. This letter was published on July 4, 2013.

> Dear precious babies in the womb, I'm writing
> this letter to you, the innocent victims of abor-

tion. Please know that there are many pro-life people and organizations that are praying for you, we are fighting for your lives. There are so many moms and dads who would love to adopt you, who are on a long waiting list in hopes of adopting a baby just like you.

I'm telling you this because I am so heart-broken and ashamed of how pro-choice people are acting. I read an article in Monday's paper about Wendy Davis, the Democratic State Senator "whose filibuster against Texas abortion restrictions gained her national fame." She said "she has been fielding congratulatory calls from around the world since her marathon filibuster." I am sick to my stomach, thinking about people doing "high fives" because you, the unborn, can still be aborted after twenty weeks. Do these people hear the words that are coming out of their mouths? I assume that these same people realize that your mother is five months pregnant at twenty weeks, and that a sonogram will show if you are a baby boy, or a baby girl, a son or a daughter. I am so sorry that women and men have made you their political stepping stone, their so called rise to fame.

The sad, ugly irony is that these same political figures scream about how the discrimination and bullying has got to stop, yet your life will end because of their discrimination against you, you are not old enough, not big enough. They

are the biggest hypocrites of all. They are afraid
to stand up for you because it's just not politi-
cally correct it's not the popular thing to do.

Today I make a vow to you, the innocent babies
in the womb, I will not be silent I will not give
up.

I will continue to pray that your mothers and
fathers see what a gift from God you truly are.
As a pro-life Catholic I have never voted for any-
one who is pro-choice, and I never will. Sweet
tiny babies in your mother's womb, I will fight
for you, I will weep for you, I will pray for you
until I draw my last breath. I am woman hear
me roar—Wendy Davis does not speak for me!

That filibuster, that letter I wrote in response, is one of the
reasons I started my blog. I'm not a political figure, not anybody
important, but I have a voice, and I made a vow to the unborn. My
blog, the posts I write, come from my heart and is the only way I
know how to try and reach people, to try and make a difference.

The final point I want to comment on is the one from this
week's article about winning a pair of pink running shoes like the
ones Wendy Davis wore during her filibuster. The appropriate color
should be red, the color of blood.

Sweet tiny babies in your mother's womb, I will fight for you.
I will speak up for you. I will do my best to help others see, the only
pink or blue running shoes should be for your precious tiny feet.

Friday, June 27, 2014

Hello out there! I have been so busy with my grandkids this week I haven't had a chance to blog,

although I have posted a couple of links to the letters I had published in the newspaper. I also posted a couple of pictures! I have a lot to say about the Wendy Davis filibuster anniversary celebration, but that will have to wait another day or two. The article I read in today's paper about her speech almost did me in, but I'll write my opinion after I've recouped from my wonderful week with my babies! I need to get some sleep. Tomorrow will be another nonstop day! I just wanted to write a quick post so that y'all wouldn't think I had given up! Thanks to everyone who takes the time to read my blog! Have a great weekend!

My motto for today is, "Promote adoption for the precious human babies. Speak up for the unborn. We are their voice. We have to fight for them!"

"The Lord is good, a refuge in times of trouble. He cares for those who trust in him" (Nahum 1:7).

Monday, June 30, 2014

Hello out there! I hope everyone had a great weekend. Ours was action packed! On Saturday, all of our children and grandchildren were with us. Since all three of our children are married, we are double blessed and now have six children and eight grandchildren. When you add my husband and me, that adds up to a bunch! We had a lot of really good food (we barbecued), plenty for everyone. I especially love when we say grace before we eat. Hearing my grandkids sweet voices as they pray is such a beautiful sound.

My motto at mealtime is, "If you are still hungry when you leave, it is your own fault." Thank you, Jesus. We always have more than enough no matter how many people stop by. I love to cook and bake. Taking care of my family is my top priority! My grandkids love to help me bake. I have so many great pictures of them in the kitchen with me.

I had my two granddaughters who live out of town with me all week. Our oldest son and daughter-in-law drove in late Friday night. They all left yesterday (Sunday) morning. We had a lot of fun last week. They enjoyed playing with all of their cousins!

Swimming, baking, playing outside, watering the flowers, coloring, going to the park and to the donut shop, and a tee-ball game were just a few of our adventures! All my grandkids love the Junie B. Jones audio cassettes or tapes or whatever they are, and we listen to them while we are in the truck running errands. I enjoy listening to them with my kiddos, and we laugh a lot. My husband, on the other hand, is not as impressed. He thinks Junie B. Jones needs a good swat, but since the kids love them, being the wonderful Pa that he is, he grins and bears it!

I so enjoy having my family all here, but I have to admit, I am tired today! Thanks for reading my blog. I hope your life is filled with love and laughter!

Bye for now.
Sharla

We sing this song at Mass, and it is one of my favorites!

"Lead me, Lord. Lead me, Lord, by the light of truth to seek and to find the narrow way. Be my way. Be my truth. Be my life, my Lord, and lead me, Lord, today!"

Wednesday, July 2, 2014

Good morning out there! For those of you who have been read-ing my posts, you know that I started my blog to help people find the information they may need or to share it with someone who needs it.

Being pro-life means a lot of things to me. I care about people. I want to help people. I want to be a voice for the unborn because they cannot speak for themselves. I want to be an advocate for them. I also care about their mothers, and I want them to know that there are life options that are not talked about enough. To be able to help people, I feel like they have to know what you stand for and that you are knowledgeable about the information they are seeking. I have a lot of pro-life links and resources on my blog so that information about adoption, pregnancy help centers, and post-abortion healing for women and men is easy to access.

I finally got a Facebook page a couple of weeks ago. Being on Facebook has been an eye-opening experience for me. I love seeing pictures of my family and friends. I enjoy hearing about their lives. I've posted some pro-life information, but I feel more comfortable writing about pro-life issues on my blog. It just seems more personal. I know that sounds crazy because anyone can see it, but I also realize that those of you who read my posts read them because you want to.

I have a bunch of pro-life T-shirts that I wear. One says, "Pro-Life to the Max" in front. Another one says, "Choose Life." I have one that says, "Life Guard," with a cross between the words that has the precious baby feet on the cross. Most of these shirts say things about protecting the unborn, helping pregnant mothers, etc., on the back. I proudly wear these shirts because the sayings on these shirts are what I believe, and they are what I stand for. I also have a bumper sticker on my truck that says, "Pro Woman, Pro Child, Pro-Life." You are probably wondering why I'm telling you this. Well, it is because I'm always ready to answer questions if people say something about my shirt or my bumper sticker, and people have.

I received a phone call the other day from someone who got my name and number from someone else because they told them I would have the information they were looking for. I felt so humbled when I spoke to this person. I was so thankful that they called me. I gave them all the information I had. This just re-emphasized how important it is to let people know what you believe in.

I pray that God will always give me the courage to stand up for what I believe in no matter where I am and on all social networking sites. The main definition of being pro-life to me means love, and babies are love; they just need to be loved.

Bye for now.
Sharla

"Do not be conformed to this world, but be transformed by the renewing of your minds, so that you may discern what is the will of God-what is good and acceptable and perfect" (Romans 12:2).

"We cannot help conforming ourselves to what we love" St. Francis de Sales)

Tuesday, July 15, 2014

What if? What if we promoted the pro-life message in such a way that everyone got it? That everyone understood that a baby is a baby, not a choice. That even though abortions are legal, no one would choose to have one. That an abortionist would see that he or she is taking a life instead of saving a life. That instead of being called an abortionist, they would want to be called a doctor. You are probably thinking, "Dream on, sister," and maybe, probably, you are right. I just know that right now, I feel an urgency about spreading the pro-life message. Maybe it is because of the elections coming up in November, I don't know. I just want to spread awareness about the help that is out there. I want people to know that abortion is not their only option. I placed brochures about adoption in our church vestibule last week. I also carry them with me. In the early morning hours, my husband and I pray for the unborn on the East Coast because we know that abortions are already in progress. We pray throughout the day for all the unborn everywhere, for their mothers and for their fathers to say *no* to abortion and *yes* to life! We pray that the abortionists will walk out and say, "No more. I will not take another baby's life, not today, not ever!" Please pray with us for the unborn. Please pray for the baby girl or baby boy's mother and father. Please pray for the abortionists. Please pray for an end to abortion.

"And when the angel had come to her, he said, 'Hail, full of grace, the Lord is with thee. Blessed art thou among women' (Luke 1:28).

"Elizabeth was filled with the Holy Spirit and cried out in a loud voice: 'Blest are you among women and blest is the fruit of your womb'" (Luke 1:41–42).

Jesus, protect and save the unborn!

Wednesday, July 23, 2014

Good morning out there! Life is precious, and not only do I pray for the unborn, I pray for those in war-torn countries. Starting my blog has been an amazing experience for me. I'm able to see the different countries that people are from who read my posts. It doesn't specify cities, but it does list how many people from each country have viewed my blog. I'm humbled that anyone would read my blog.

People from Russia and Ukraine have been reading my blog, but I haven't seen either country listed in over two weeks. Because of all the fighting that is going on, I'm worried about them. I hope that they are okay. I just want them to know that I am praying for them and for their families. I don't know their names. I don't know what they look like, but for some reason, they read my blog. Each day I don't see their country listed, I place my hand over the map where it should be colored in, and I pray for them.

There are so many wars going on in our world right now, so much violence.

Dear God, please watch over all these countries where war has broken out. Please, God, protect the innocent people and their families. Please, God, open their government's eyes to the devastation that war is causing. Please, God, guide their leaders to a peaceful solution. Thank you, God, for our many blessings. Please be with all those who are in need. Please, God, show us and guide us to how we can best help others. You created us all. Please help us to love our neighbor, care for one another, and pray for those who seek a better life. In Jesus's name I pray, dear Lord, amen.

As Catholics, we pray The Divine Mercy Chaplet. This prayer is for the whole world. It is really beautiful when we sing this chaplet. (I'm singing this as I'm typing.) The refrain goes like this: "For the sake of His sorrowful passion, have mercy on us and on the whole world."

If you listen to the Catholic radio station, 91.5 FM, they sing the Divine Mercy Chaplet at 3:00 p.m. each day.

To pray The Chaplet of Divine Mercy (it is easier to keep up with if you have a rosary, but if you don't, you can count on your fingers),

1. Begin with the sign of the cross, pray (1) Our Father, (1) Hail Mary, and The Apostles Creed.
2. Prayer: (Pray this once) "Eternal Father, I offer You the body and blood, soul and divinity of Your dearly beloved Son, Our Lord Jesus Christ, in atonement for our sins and those of the whole world."
3. Pray this refrain ten times: "For the sake of His sorrowful passion, have mercy on us and on the whole world." You repeat steps 2 and 3 for a total of five times.
4. Conclude with (thrice) "Holy God, Holy Mighty One, Holy Immortal One, have mercy on us and on the whole world."
5. The sign of the cross and amen.

It is a beautiful, peaceful prayer. I find myself humming or singing it a lot. I also pray it if I wake up during the night.

May God bless you and keep you safe wherever you are, wherever you live. May God help us to love and care for each other.

Blessings and peace.
Sharla

July 28, 2014

The world we live in today believes that a woman's choice is more important than a baby's life, and that is a lie. The world we live in today believes "Live and let live," unless you are a baby in your mother's womb. If you are pregnant, there are two lives to think about now, two lives to take care of. Please, choose life for your baby. I've talked to women who are still devastated about an abortion they had years ago. It has taken decades for some women to finally heal after an abortion. I've read articles and heard testimonials. I've cried with women as they have shared their stories with me. I write this blog not only to save the baby, but to save the young woman from the heartache and guilt she feels after having an abortion. No one wants to talk about this subject because it just isn't very comfortable. It is certainly not politically correct unless you are pro-abortion, and people just don't want to get involved. So here I am, because I truly care. I truly want to make a difference. I want to get the message out there; abortion is an ugly lie. I'm not saying that choosing adoption for your baby will be easy, and I'm also not saying that raising your baby will be easy. But I believe if you choose life for your baby. Once you hold your sweet baby boy or baby girl in your arms, you will make the right decision for both of you.

One of the definitions of mother in the dictionary is "to care for or protect as a mother does."

A baby's heart starts beating just eighteen days after conception. Listen to your heart. Place your hands over your stomach, and think about the baby boy or baby girl that is growing inside you. That tiny little life is a miracle and needs you. Listen to your heart. Don't listen to the world. You are strong enough to take care of your baby, and if you choose adoption, you are doing what you feel like is best for your baby. Please choose life for your baby. There are people out there who will help you.

"For I know well the plans I have for you, declares the Lord, plans for welfare and not for woe to give you a future and a hope" (Jeremiah 29:11).

Thursday, August 14, 2014

Good morning out there! I am continually picking up brochures, handouts, and other pro-life resources to share with you. I was excited to read the two articles I've listed below. I want to be able to share these resources if someone asks me, "How do you know this?" or "Where did you hear that?" I want people to understand that what I write about in my blog is not just my opinion. Yes, many things I write about are how I feel about abortion. Since I was adopted at birth, I do write about my feelings on adoption being a loving option. I also write about heart-wrenching, post-abortive testimonials that I've heard first-hand and testimonials I have read about. I realize that all these things are what different people think or feel, and I view all these as very important. But sometimes, you talk to people who don't care about feelings. They don't care about emotions. They want scientific proof. To some people, a sonogram, the amazing illustration of gestational stages of a baby's development, is not enough. So when I come across articles like the ones below, I definitely want to share them. I hope that articles like these will help people who need to hear this information from a scientific point of view. Maybe they will change their mind and see that a baby is a baby. Maybe it will help some people who are pro-life but aren't sure about speaking up. Give them a voice. Sadly, there will still be some people who will say it doesn't matter, that a woman's choice is still more important than the life of the innocent baby boy or baby girl that the mother carries in her womb.

I will continue to write about any and all pro-life information I come across. I will continue to speak out, to speak up for those who cannot speak for themselves. I hope you enjoy the articles. Please pass them on.

I hope you all have a great day filled with many blessings! Thanks for reading my blog.

Bye for now.

Sharla

Dr. Alfred M. Bongiovanni, professor of pediatrics and obstetrics at the University of Pennsylvania, stated,

"I have learned from my earliest medical education that human life begins at the time of conception...I submit that human life is present throughout this entire sequence from conception to adulthood and that any interruption at any point throughout this time constitutes a termination of human life...

I am no more prepared to say that these early stages [of development in the womb] represent an incomplete human being than I would be to say that the child prior to the dramatic effects of puberty...is not a human being. This is human life at every stage."

Read more: http://www.epm.org/resources/2010/Mar/8/scientists-attest-life-beginning-conception/#ixzz3AHny7v9F

Dr. Jerome LeJeune, professor of genetics at the University of Descartes in Paris, was the discoverer of the chromosome pattern of Down syndrome. Dr. LeJeune testified to the Judiciary Subcommittee, "after fertilization has taken place a new human being has come into being." He stated that this "is no longer a matter of taste or opinion," and "not a metaphysical contention, it is plain experimental evidence."

He added, "Each individual has a very neat beginning, at conception."

Read more:
http://www.epm.org/resources/2010/Mar/8/scientists-attest-life-beginning-conception/#ixzz3AHny7v9F

Monday, August 25, 2014

Hello out there! I just wanted to share something that touched my heart last night during Mass. I was a lector and a Eucharistic minister, so I was up by the altar and able to see everyone all the way to the back of the cathedral. What caught my eye was my son holding his fourteen-month-old daughter, and my daughter holding her twenty-eight-month-old daughter standing next to each other right below the statue of St. Anthony. Sacred Heart Cathedral has been our parish home for more than thirty-one years. Last night, while my son, daughter, and two of my granddaughters were at the back of the cathedral, another one of my granddaughters (my daughter's oldest) was an altar server for the first time. She was up near the altar with me. My husband is an usher, so he was standing by the side doors as people were receiving Communion. As my daughter-in-law and our other three grandchildren passed by my husband, she was the only one who sat down. The kids stopped and stood right next to Pa as unofficial ushers. My son-in-law was standing in the back. Our oldest son and his family live in the Houston area, but they were with us in thoughts and prayers. As a matter of fact, we lit two candles after Mass last night, one for each of the girls, because they started school today. The youngest one is now in kindergarten and was a little apprehensive. I told her on the phone yesterday before church that we would light a candle for them and pray for them to have a good day and a good week.

When my husband and I were driving home (by ourselves), we laughed about how great it is when the kids are at Mass!

I remember when my son and daughter used to be altar servers themselves, and when I looked out and saw them standing side by side, each holding a wiggly, squiggly little girl in their arms, I just thought, it doesn't get much better than this! Thank you, God.

Thank you. Thank you for my many blessings. I am so grateful for my family. I am so grateful for my life. I love you God, Amen.

Have a great day! Bye for now.
Sharla

God's Prayerful People

Tuesday, September 16, 2014

Hello out there! It's a beautiful overcast day here in San Angelo, TX. We were blessed with rain overnight. We are always thankful for the rain out here! I just got home from helping out with the Sack Lunch Ministry. Our parish, Sacred Heart Cathedral, provides for the homeless and other people in need. Our parish is in the downtown area, and we give out sack lunches Monday through Friday from 11:30 a.m. to 1:00 p.m. We fed a lot of people today. We gave out over eighty sack lunches. You never know how many people will stop by. We usually hand out between forty to eighty lunches a day. In the summer, we hand out more because kids are home from school. Everyone is always so appreciative. I only help out twice a month. Some of the other volunteers are there almost every day. After we cleaned up and locked the doors, I went over to the parish office and visited with the secretary about the details for the kick-off rally we'll have next Wednesday evening for the 40 Days for Life Campaign. I bought two candles and walked over to the sanctuary. I love being in the sanctuary during the day when no one else is in there. There is no way to describe the peace I feel when I kneel down to pray. It's so quiet in there. Light comes through the stained glass windows, and it's beautiful. I look up at the huge crucifix hanging on the wall behind the altar, a reminder that my Jesus died on the cross for all our sins. I walked down the side isle towards the back, where the shrine to Our Lady of Guadalupe is. I was going to light my candles and say a prayer, but I noticed that all the candle holders were already full. I smiled and sat my candles on the floor and knelt down on the kneeler. When I saw all those candles burning, it was a visual image to me of faith. Every person lit a candle and knelt down and asked Mother Mary to pray for their special need, who lifted up their prayer to God. What a beautiful sign of faith. I prayed for everyone who lit a candle. I prayed for my family, and then I softly sang the "Hail Mary" so overcome with emotion and the peace I felt at that moment. God is always with us. Sometimes we need to step out and away from all the noise in today's world to feel His presence. I'm so thankful that I took the time to spend a few quiet minutes alone with God and was able to witness the faith of His prayerful people.

I brought my candles home with me. They'll be lit later on, and every time I pass by and see the flicker of the light, a prayer of peace for all of you, whether near or far, will be on lips and in my heart.

God bless you all.
Sharla

"Lead me, Lord. Lead me, Lord, by the light of truth, to seek and to find the narrow way. Be my way. Be my truth. Be my life my, Lord, and lead me, Lord, today."

Prayers for the Whole World

Friday, October 3, 2014

Hello out there! I miss posting on my blog! I've been so busy with the 40 Days for Life Campaign I just haven't had any extra time! A really quick post to say hello, and I hope you are all doing well.

Please know that we are praying for families all over the whole world. We are praying for the unborn, we are praying for mothers and fathers, and we are praying for those whose lives are torn apart because of the terrorist attacks and hostile takeovers. I pray that God will keep all of you safe. I pray that God will protect your families. I pray for an end to war.

I pray for an end to abortion.

So many people have been coming out to pray. Some come every day. Some spend hours in prayer, lifting you up. I know that people from other countries read my blog. I'm praying for you. We are all lifting you up in prayer during these 40 Days.

Blessings to all. I have to get back to the courtyard and pray!

Bye for now.
Sharla

"Mercy, peace and love be yours in abundance" (Jude 1:2).

"The Lord is close to the brokenhearted and saves those who are crushed in spirit" (Psalm 34:18).

"Enter into the inner chamber of your mind. Shut out all things save God and whatever may aid you in seeking God; and having barred the door of your chamber, seek Him" (St. Anselm of Canterbury).

Growing up Pro-Life

Prayers, Faith, and Peace

Wednesday, October 8, 2014

Hello out there! Is anybody still reading my blog? I'm sorry that I haven't written very many posts lately. I've been so busy with our 40 Days for Life Campaign I just haven't had much spare time. When I do have some spare time, I have to do things like wash clothes, cook, do some paperwork for our family business, you know, that kind of stuff that is never ending! Anyway, I just want to share with y'all how amazing the first fifteen days of the 40-day campaign have been. So many people have been coming out to the courtyard and praying. It has been such a blessing for me to see all these faithful people. Some people pray in groups, some people pray by themselves, but there is always so much joy. Smiling faces, hugs, faith sharing, laughter, quiet time, peacefulness, and, most of all, the love and presence of Jesus Christ. People of all ages have come out to pray. Mothers with small children who color on the concrete with sidewalk chalk. Couples, sisters, rosary groups, families, friends, the list goes on and on. When a new person shows up, they are immediately welcomed to our growing family of people who pray for the unborn, who pray for families, who pray for the whole world. We are united in our belief that life begins at conception, that babies are a gift from God, and our faith in God. Each day, I am blessed with the witness of these faithful people.

Right now, something else has been on my heart and on the hearts of many of those who come and pray. We are worried about those of you in countries that are at war. We are praying for you and your families.

I can't imagine what you are dealing with, what you are going through. I pray that all of you who live in war-torn countries are safe and cared for. I pray that no harm comes to you or those you love. I pray for peace for your countries. I pray for guidance and leadership for my country and yours. I listen to the news, and I know that a lot of innocent people are living in fear and worse. It may not seem like much, but I lit a candle at church today and prayed for all of you. When I wake up during the night, I pray for you.

Please know that wherever you are, we are praying for you daily during this 40 Days for Life Campaign. We are lifting you up in our prayers. Peace be with you. God's blessings to you and yours.

Please, God, have mercy on us and on the whole world. Please protect the innocent. Please take care of families. Please have mercy on us all. Amen.

There Are Angels among Us, Sent Down to Us from God Above

Friday, October 24, 2014

Good morning out there! It is extremely early, 4:15 a.m. to be exact, but I can't sleep! How are y'all doing? Today is day 31 of the fall 40 Days for Life Campaign. Only nine days left! So many blessings! I want to list some of the many blessings that I see and experience each day. I'm touched by angels every day. God is so great! I wish that I had taken the time to list one recap of each day as it happened. But since I didn't, here are just some of the blessings I've received during this pro-life prayer campaign.

On weekdays, we have an average of thirty-two people a day come and pray. On the weekends, the average is about twenty people a day (give or take a little). Some of these people come daily; some come multiple times a week. Some pop in for twenty to thirty minutes. Others stay for an hour, and then there are those who spend two hours or more. One of my friends, Irma, is at the courtyard at 7:00 a.m. Mondays to Fridays and comes back again at 3:00 p.m. (When the church bells ring at three, we sing the Divine Mercy Chaplet). Needless to say, she is an angel and a dear friend. She has also brought me an apple and a granola bar because she was worried I wasn't eating! She has also sent me home and stayed longer! Since she is there at seven, I don't have to be there until eight!

Another one of my friends, Muriel, comes daily. She fills in when I need her (a lot). She also comes at 7:00 a.m. on Sunday mornings and stays until right before Mass at 10:00 a.m. She then comes back at 5:45 p.m. and closes up at 7:00 p.m. so that my husband and I can go to the 6:00 p.m. Mass. She is another angel and dear friend. My friend, Candi, will show up and say, "Go home, Sharla. You need a break! I've got you covered!" She has done this several times. She also brought me an apple, washed and cut in half, in a baggie! We pray together, visit, and always end up in tears! She always shows up just when I need her most. Another angel. Another dear friend.

There are many more who send me on my way, so many special people I am blessed to spend time with almost each and every day. We have this common bond, our love of God, our faith, our pro-life stance, our commitment to speaking up for the unborn. Last but definitely not least is my own family: my wonderful husband, my children, and my grandchildren. They are so supportive. They come and pray. They help close up so that I can go on home. They under-stand when I'm tired, and for the last thirty-one days, they've done everything they can to make my life easier since I spend so much time at the courtyard. They never complain and love to hear about the many blessings of prayer and fellowship I've been a part of that day.

I hope you all have a wonderful day, full of blessings and angels! I am going to go and get ready to start my day at the courtyard! I will need lots of coffee today! Really, I just need God's grace, His love, His angels. I need Him!

Bye for now.
Sharla

"From his fullness we have all received, grace upon grace" (John 1:16).

Guardian Angel

Riley

40 Days of Prayer, Fellowship, and Blessings!

Tuesday, November 4, 2014

Good morning out there! The fall 40 Days for Life Campaign is over! I received an e-mail from the 40 Days headquarters letting me know that 546 babies were saved during this campaign! Isn't that amazing? I'm so thankful for all the people who took the time to go and pray. I can only imagine what these young ladies are thinking when they are taken to an abortion facility. I'm so glad that there were people who care standing outside in prayer, telling them that there is help available. We don't have an abortion facility where I live. The Planned Parenthood closed down in September 2013. They did not do surgical abortions, but they did give out the pill that would cause a chemical abortion. We used to pray in front of the Planned Parenthood during the 40 Days for Life Campaigns until it closed down. We still wanted to be involved and found out that we could still have a campaign in our city as long as it was outside, where we would be visible.

Our campaign was held in the courtyard of our parish, Sacred Heart Cathedral. Our vigil hours were from 7:00 a.m. to 7:00 p.m. each and every day from Wednesday, September 24 through Sunday, November 2, 2014. We had many people come and pray throughout the days of the campaign. Several people came four and five times a week. Some people came daily. Many stayed and prayed for more than an hour at a time. We had rosary groups come and pray in the courtyard. People would stay and visit after their prayers or devotions. It was an amazing time of fellowship. We came together to pray for the unborn, for their families, for the whole world. The courtyard used to be a place we walked through to get inside the school building. It has now become a place of prayer, a peaceful place where you feel the Holy Spirit. You can feel God's presence there. Time just seemed to slip by as you prayed. You never felt alone there, even if you were the only one there.

The big oak trees gave us shade. The daily visits from a squirrel, the birds singing—our courtyard has become a peaceful place of prayer!

We did have trouble with pesky mosquitoes! They were vicious! We kept bottles of repellant on the table! But those mosquitoes were a small nuisance! The blessings we all received from the devotion to our prayers are indescribable. My life will never be the same. I will hold forever in my heart the beautiful, humbling witness of God's faithful people coming together in prayer. New friendships were made, and there was a closer bond with old friends, the joy of worship, and the joy of fellowship!

At the beginning of the 40 Days for Life Campaign, we would pray the Divine Mercy Chaplet together when the church bells would ring at 3:00 p.m. Midway through the campaign, we would tentatively sing the chaplet, and towards the end, we would sing with confidence, knowing that our voices lifted up as one made a beautiful melody, a song of praise to our God. One day last week, when I had gone home, the ladies shared with me that while they were singing the Divine Mercy Chaplet, a man was standing outside the courtyard, listening to them. The ladies stopped singing before they started the next decade to ask him if he needed something, if they could help him. He replied that he didn't want to disturb them, that the song was so beautiful. He explained what he needed, and then they finished singing the Divine Mercy Chaplet. As I'm writing this post, I can hear the rain pouring outside. We had beautiful weather during the campaign. Here in West Texas, rain is always a welcome blessing. I thank God for the rain and for the babies saved. I pray for the families of these babies, that they will be given the guidance and help they need.

I thank God for all the people who participated in 40 Days for Life Campaigns everywhere. Blessings to you all!

Bye for now.
Sharla

O Lord, I am not worthy. Thank you for my many blessings. Amen.

Team Work – 40 Days for Life Campaigns

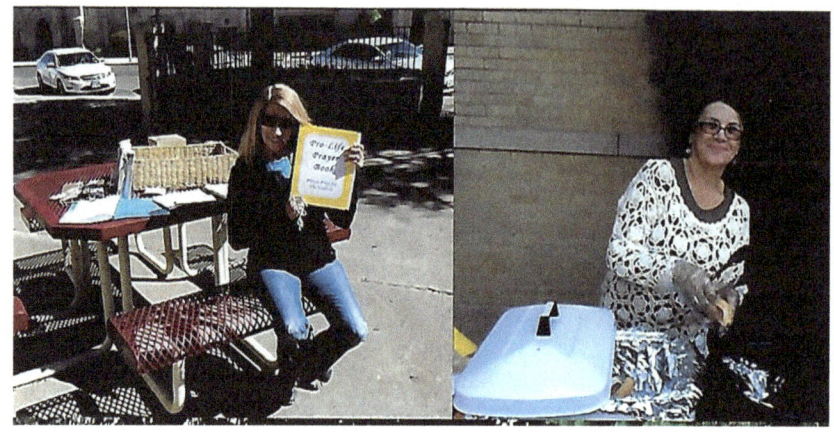

Working Together and Having Fun

Trying to Be a Light
in This Dark World

Thursday, November 5, 2015

Hello out there! Just a quick post. Yesterday, at the Sack Lunch Ministry, a young man showed up early. We had never seen him before. He sat in the cafeteria with his head down while he was waiting for us to start handing out lunches. I walked by him and hollered out something to the ladies in the kitchen. He misunderstood what I said and became defensive. I immediately walked over to him and sat down next to him. I told him that he misunderstood, and then I asked him what his name was. He told me his name, and then I told him mine and reached out my hand to shake his. We talked for about ten minutes. He isn't from here, and the lost look in his eyes broke my heart. I gave him his lunch and told him to go out to the courtyard and I would send someone to visit with him. I had just dropped by to leave supplies. It wasn't my day to stay and help, and I had an appointment. I went out the back door and climbed into my truck and said a quick prayer. It went something like this: "Okay, Lord, how am I supposed to help this young man? Lord, there are so many people in pain. How do we help them? Amen." I called one of the deacons and asked if he would stop by the courtyard on his way to the noon Mass. He said that he would. I drove around the block and pulled into a parking space in front of the courtyard. I got some money out of my purse and walked to the courtyard. He was sitting on a bench eating his sandwich. I sat down next to him and told him that if he would just wait for a little while, that someone would be by to talk to him. I handed him the money and told him that it should be enough to get some dinner later on. I stood up to leave, and he stood up also. He gave me a hug and thanked me. He told me that he was sorry he had gotten upset earlier, and I told him that I was sorry I hadn't just sat down to talk to him in the first place! I don't know what happened after I left. I hope he is okay. I prayed for him and all those who are like him with nowhere to go. I told my husband last night that I feel like we are living in a time where the whole world is like a field hospital. Some people just need a hug or a smile, and it is easy to fix them right up. Others need so much more. I told Jim that I feel like we just walk around with Band-Aids trying to make it all better, and sometimes, they need major surgery. I just feel so inadequate sometimes. I pray that God will always guide me to know what to do, to know how to help. I just know one thing for sure: we have to be a light in this dark world.

I just needed to share this. My heart is sad. God bless you all. Please be a light to others!

Bye for now.
Sharla

Let My Little Light Shine!

Friday, November 6, 2015

Good morning out there! Yesterday, I wrote a post about something that had happened at the Sack Lunch Ministry the day before. After I wrote the post, I started thinking and was praying as I went about my morning. This is what happened next.

After I finished writing, I went into the kitchen to fix lunch for my husband so that I could take it to where he was working. My mind kept going back to that young man and to so many others that I have met at the Sack Lunch Ministry. I just wanted to cry. My heart felt so heavy. I started praying as I packed up Jim's lunch and loaded everything into my truck. By the time I reached Jim, I had realized something. It was like a light had turned on. I couldn't wait to share it with him. Jim climbed into the passenger side of the truck, and I said, "I figured it out! I know what God is telling us!" Jim had that look on his face that said, "Oh my gosh, what has she gotten us into now?" I told him about my blog post and how I wanted to cry and how my heart hurt. I told him how I prayed and asked God what we were supposed to do because we can only do so much. And then it hit me like a ton of bricks, because I'm hard-headed, and that is usually the only way God can get through to me. I felt like God was saying, "Yes, y'all are working in the field hospital, providing food, hugs, smiles, and kind words. Sometimes you provide clothing and information and sometimes money. The bandages that you provide are needed, and then you pray and I [God] will take care of the operations, the major stuff." I realized that God just wants us to be faithful, to do what we are able, and, most importantly, to do something. I think about all the darkness in this world, and if I am a light and you are a light and if others will be a light, just think about how God's love will shine in us and through us!

There is a song we sing in Mass called "We Are Many Parts," and it is one of my favorite songs. The refrain goes like this: "We are many parts, we are all one body, and the gifts we have we are given to share. May the Spirit of love make us one indeed; one, the love that we share, one, our hope in despair, one the cross that we bear."

My plan for today is to go out and let my little light shine!

Blessings to you and yours.

Sharla

Reflection and Thanksgiving

Tuesday, November 18, 2014

Good morning out there! I hope that everyone is doing well and staying warm! It is 23 degrees right now (8:20 a.m.), but the sun is shining, and it looks like it is going to be a beautiful day! I'm getting back into my old routine now that the 40 Days for Life Campaign is over. Though I have to admit, I miss the daily fellowship! However, I have enjoyed sitting by the fireplace, with a roaring fire, on these cold days! I was way behind on the book work for our family business, so I have been busy catching up. On the cold days, I dragged the little table my grandkids use when they are coloring, working puzzles, and eating their snacks on over by the fireplace and worked! Of course, when everyone comes over, I have to move all my stuff back into my office!

It has been so cold at night that we have let our dogs come inside to sleep. They are a mess. Stormy is an English bulldog, and Bella is three quarter Blue Healer and a quarter Australian Shepherd. They are both really good dogs, very protective of me and the grandkids! We have tiled floors in our home, and there is a red throw rug between the kitchen and living room. Both of the "girls" were on the rug this morning, and Jim was trying to come into the kitchen to eat. He had to step over them because they were not moving! We both laughed. They are so funny!

I don't know if I told y'all that my daughter and her husband are expecting another baby, a little girl, due in the spring. We are all excited. This makes three little girls for them! Their oldest daughter is eight, and she is very practical. When they found out the baby is a sister, she said, "Well, that's good, because we are prepared for a girl. We have all girl stuff already!" Their youngest is two and a half, and she sings to her mommy's tummy and tells us where the baby is!

My son and his wife are also expecting in the spring. If everyone stays on schedule, the babies will be born about a week apart! They have two boys and two girls. This baby will be the tiebreaker! They are waiting until the baby is born to find out if this one is a brother or a sister! The boys want a brother, the girls want a sister, but really and truly, they are just excited about having another sibling. Jim and I are excited about our new grandbabies! Our oldest son (my stepson) and his wife have two girls. I dreamed that she was also expecting but was informed that it was just a dream! Jim and I are very blessed to have ten grandchildren now! Even though we won't be able to hold two of them until the spring, they are already loved and prayed for, already a big part of our growing family. Last week, I was with my daughter and her family when they did the sonogram. There is no way to adequately describe how amazing it is to see my newest granddaughter's development, her little nose and how she placed her hand over her knee while we were watching. I'm just so thankful. I feel so blessed.

Well, I better get busy. I have a lot to accomplish today. I think I'm also going to make some oatmeal cookies with chocolate chips in them! I'm still trying to figure out what I'm going to fix the guys for lunch (my husband and son come home for lunch most days). I've got the dessert figured out though!

I hope you all have a wonderful day filled with many blessings!

I'm going to close with a prayer written by Cardinal Newman.

"Dear Lord, shine through me, and be so in me that every soul I come in contact with may feel Your Presence in my soul…Let me thus praise you in the way you love best, by shining on those around me. Amen."

Every Baby Should Be able to Grow Up and Have a Story to Tell

Friday, December 5, 2014

Once upon a time, fifty or so years ago, a baby girl was born, and she needed a home. Never knowing the circumstances or the reason her birth mother couldn't keep her, she had to say good-bye. This little baby girl was three days old when a loving family came and took her to their home. Now this baby girl had a family of her own.

With love and joy and happiness, this baby girl grew up. She never met a stranger, and her heart was full of love. She loved to hear the stories about her special day, the day her family came and gave her their name.

When she was only eight years old, the scary news came: her loving mother had cancer. The little girl was afraid. Her mother was strong and courageous as she battled day to day, and when the girl was but twelve years old, the angels came and took her mother away. She knew her mother was in heaven; no more pain did she feel, and although she understood why it had to be this way, the grief she felt in her heart would never go away. The young, not-quite-teenage girl was strong; she was raised that way. She had watched her mother suffer and never heard her complain. Her mother had prepared her, knowing this day would come. Her love of God, her father, older brother, church family, and friends would be there for her as the years came and went. She was now a young lady, thought she was so grown up. Off she went to college—another life event. She made new friends, and she had fun, but she missed her dad, her brother, his wife, and friends back home.

Then one day it happened, a Sunday afternoon, she met a man, the most wonderful, handsome man, and her heart grew and grew. Within a short time, they were married, became husband and wife. So thankful God had blessed her with someone she would cherish and love all of her life. She had a new name and a home of her own. She was also blessed with a stepson she quickly grew to love as her very own.

Expecting their first child, the baby grew, and as the mother heard the heartbeat and felt her baby move, she was amazed at what her body was going through. With her husband by her side, the doctor said, "It's a boy," and the mother cried. "My firstborn is a son." And the emotions that went through her can never be described, but the love and protectiveness she felt for this child was an overwhelming feeling that would never die. As she held her son close to her breast, she thanked God for his life, for being so blessed. When the baby boy was just three months old, the new mom found out she was expecting once more. When her husband came home from work that day, he sat down in the rocking chair and held their son. She knelt on the floor and leaned against his legs as she shared the good news of another baby on the way. He smiled and told her everything would be okay.

This happened during the time when the oil boom had gone bust, work was slow, there had been lay-offs, and his new job didn't pay as much. There would be no insurance to cover the costs. They saved and worked side jobs to pay for the birth. The hard times together—they grew so close.

The baby boy walked at ten months old, and his mom chased after him as her other baby began to grow. The mother heard the heartbeat and felt her baby move, and once more, she was amazed at what her body was going through. The baby boy was happy and had a beautiful smile. He was into everything, and his pregnant mom was tired! Would this new baby be a brother or a sister for the two boys they already had? Another son or a daughter—either way, they would be glad! The night before the baby came, the mom was in the kitchen. She looked into the living room just in time to see her baby boy dive from the chair into the presents beneath the Christmas tree. She dashed across the floor and caught him midair, nine months pregnant, not a moment to spare!

Early the next morning, the labor pains came. They picked up their sleepy baby boy, and all loaded up in the black pickup truck. They took him to his aunt and uncles and told him they'd be back, and off to the hospital they dashed. Just four hours later, with her husband by her side, they heard the doctor say, "It's a girl!" And then they cried. Tears of joy—a daughter, a baby girl—and the emotions that went through her can never be described, but the love and protectiveness she felt for this child was an overwhelming feeling that would never die. As she held her daughter close to her breast, she thanked God for her life, for being so blessed.

The next year was busy with two babies under two. The baby boy was fearless and loved to run and climb. The baby girl was carried upon her mother's hip to keep her off the floor and safe from baby brother who would zoom back and forth. The baby girl was happy and loved her mom and dad. She would laugh at her brother's antics and stay close by her mama's side. She loved her swing, and you can guess why; the floor was otherwise occupied! The years went by, and the children grew up. They loved when their son came for a visit, their family complete. They were a close-knit family and shared so much love. They were raised going to Mass and all their sacraments they made. God was always a priority and still is to this day.

Three weddings have been celebrated and blessings of grandbabies galore. Who could ask for anything more?

Yes, it's true. This story is about me and my sweet and amazing family. I seem to get nostalgic this time of year. My son and daughter both have birthdays this month. They were both born on Fridays, and it was cold and had snowed both years. I remember Jim driving us home in our old black pickup truck. There was a Christmas tree in the living room to welcome us as we stepped in.

Their birthdays are right before Christmas, and mine is right after. We celebrate the birth of Jesus right between our birthdays. Yes, December is a special month for us! I think back to the years when I was pregnant and how we got things ready for the birth of our babies. It makes me think of how Advent is a time of waiting, of preparation. Having been adopted at birth, I don't take life for granted. Life is a gift, and we are all beautifully, fearfully, wonderfully made. Every baby should be able to grow up and have a story to tell.

I hope you enjoyed my story! Bye for now.

Sharla

My Nativity Scene:
A Time of Preparation

Saturday, December 20, 2014

Good morning out there! I hope everyone is having a wonderful Advent! I set up my beautiful nativity scene outside on Thursday. Now I'm waiting for Christmas to place Baby Jesus in the manger. My grandkids know why I don't have Him with Mary and Joseph yet. We are still waiting for Him to come, waiting for His birth! I have hay bales stacked up on each side of my nativity scene. The baby lambs are lying up on top of one of the hay bales. After I put the nativity scene out on my front porch, I went to the grocery store. When I got back home, I saw my cat lying up on the hay bale next to the baby lambs! She must be waiting for baby Jesus too.

A couple of years ago, a porcupine would come in our yard and eat the acorns that had fallen from our oak tree. He would walk right in front of the nativity scene. One day, he was right next to the hay bale. He wanted to be with the other animals waiting for Baby Jesus! I went outside and took pictures of him. My husband hollered out the door that I was going to end up with quills in my rear if I didn't watch out! No quills in the rear, but I did get a lot of neat pictures! I'll post them so that you can see them.

I love Advent, and I love the Christmas season, but most of all, I love the reason for the season. I wish all of you joy and happiness, family time, and peace. Remember to take time to sit and have a cup of coffee, tea, or eggnog, and just enjoy the beauty of this time of year. Reach out to someone who doesn't have family. Stop by for a visit. Take a plate of cookies. Give them your time.

Blessings to you all! Happy Advent! Remember to enjoy the time of preparation!

Bye for now.
Sharla

Christmas Is More Than Just One Day!

Monday, December 29, 2014

Hello out there! I hope you all are having a wonderful Christmas! I love the entire Christmas season! We spent Christmas Eve with our children and grandchildren. We went to the Christmas Eve Vigil Mass and then came back home for food and fun! My daughter-in-law's parents and one of my son's friends from school (whom we claim as one of our own) joined us also. We have a beautiful nativity scene on the front porch. I wrapped our statue of Baby Jesus in a warm blanket and placed him in the manger, and then we sang Happy Birthday. The grandkids love that. I did have to tell them that we were not adding the "Cha Cha Cha" part as we sang to Baby Jesus!

On Christmas Day, Jim and I woke up to a quiet house! While he fixed breakfast, I ran some sugar cookies that my daughter and grandkids made up to the Sack Lunch Ministry at our church. Some really special people made sure that sack lunches were given out on Christmas Day to those in need! I delivered the cookies and gave all those sweet people a hug and wished them a Merry Christmas and headed back home. I baked a pecan pie to take to my sister-in-law's for a late lunch. We enjoyed visiting and catching up with our extended family.

On the third day of Christmas, I baked banana bread and ordered cards with pictures of my family to send out for a Happy

New Year! (Needless to say, I didn't get my Christmas cards out in time!)

On the fourth day of Christmas, I delivered banana bread to many of my neighbors. Tomorrow is my birthday! I will be fifty-one. I can't believe it!

Well, I just wanted to say hello and that I hope you are all having a blessed Christmas season! I'll try to write another post tomorrow.

I will close with this verse from the Bible: "The Lord has done great things for us, and we are filled with joy" (Psalm 126:3).

Bye for now.
Sharla

On the Sixth Day of Christmas, I Celebrate Another Year

Tuesday, December 30, 2014

Good morning out there! Today is the sixth day within the octave of the nativity of the Lord, also known as the sixth day of Christmas! I love that my birthday falls during the Christmas season! Sometimes, I'm like a small child. When I woke up today, I danced around in my flannel pajamas singing, "It's my birthday. It's my birthday!" I'm not excited because I may get presents but because I'm alive! Each day is a gift; our life is a gift from God. I want to share something from the *Magnificat* (a monthly Catholic book with the readings from the Old and New Testaments of the Bible and responsorial psalms that will be proclaimed at daily Mass). The booklet also includes morning prayers, a hymn from the scriptures, evening prayers, a meditation for the day, and a short story about the lives of certain saints. The following is from the readings for today in the *Magnificat*:

Canticle of Judith

As for me, I am old and gray. I have lived with you from my youth to the present day.

1 Samuel 12:2

Anna had grown old in faith and hope, but when she saw the Child of God's promise brought to the temple, she sang in her heart a new song of praise and thanksgiving. One is never too old to be surprised by joy.

A reading from the holy Gospel according to Luke 2:36–40

There was a prophetess, Anna, the daughter of Phanuel, of the tribe of Asher. She was advanced in years, having lived seven years with her husband after her marriage, and then as a widow until she was eighty-four. She was constantly in the temple, worshiping day and night with fasting and prayer. And coming forward at that very time, she gave thanks to God and spoke about the child to all who were awaiting the redemption of Jerusalem. When the pair had fulfilled all the prescriptions of the law of the Lord, they returned to Galilee, to their own town of Nazareth. The child grew in size and strength, filled with wisdom, and the grace of God was upon him.

Glory in his holy name;

Rejoice, O hearts that seek the Lord! Look to the Lord in his strength; seek to serve him constantly.

1 Chronicles 16:10–11

I wanted to share these readings with you because I realize how much they describe the way I feel today. So I start my new year of life today with hope, with joy, with faith, with anticipation of the days ahead, and most of all, with love in my heart and a prayer of thanksgiving on my lips.

Blessings to you all! I pray that we will all keep the true meaning of Christmas and the beautiful spirit of Christmas in our hearts and homes throughout this year and in the new year to come.

Bye for now.
Sharla

Cutest Little Percolator

Tuesday, January 6, 2015

Good morning out there! Wait, I have to go get a second cup of coffee before I begin! I'm back, with a hot cup of coffee, a little cream, and a little sugar! I was going to write about something else, but I've decided to share a neat story instead. I really enjoy drinking coffee in the morning; my husband does too. It all started with a gift I received at my bridal shower many years ago!

When Jim and I got married, I was nineteen, and he was twenty-seven. I wanted to be the perfect little housewife! I would get up and make breakfast every morning before Jim would head off to work. He has always been a welder, so oatmeal and cereal just aren't a good breakfast when you have a physically demanding job. I would fry up bacon and eggs and fix toast with butter and jelly. Well, I received the cutest little four- to six-cup percolator as a gift at my bridal shower. So every morning, I would make coffee. I remember asking Jim what he took in his coffee, and he said, "Milk and sugar."

So it began. Every morning, no matter what I cooked for breakfast, Jim and I had one or two cups of coffee. We both added milk and sugar. As the years came and went, so did the coffeemakers! Large percolators, Mr. Coffees, the percolators were my favorite because I liked the bubbly, gurgling noises they made! Jim stopped putting milk in his coffee. You never know what I want in my coffee—sometimes cream, sometimes not, always sugar (use to be Equal then Splenda, now Truvia). Anyway, no matter what we ate for breakfast,

69

we always had a cup or two of coffee! We prepare the coffee the night before and set the delayed brew button. That way, when we wake up, the coffee is ready. I always say it is like magic! I love waking up to the smell of afresh pot of coffee! We use Folgers, not the flavored foo-foo kind!

About five years ago, Jim and I were taking a walk. We were talking about all kinds of things, and we both stated that we were glad we didn't smoke cigarettes, and he was glad he had stopped dipping many years ago, and such. Anyway, Jim said the only thing we both had to have was coffee in the morning. Then he said that it was all my fault! I said, "What do you mean all my fault?" Jim replied that I made coffee every morning and set a cup for him on the table with his breakfast. So he figured I must be a big coffee drinker, and he didn't want to hurt my feelings since we had just gotten married, so he drank it! Well, I started laughing hard—you know, the kind where you double over laughing. When I stopped laughing like a hyena and got my breath back, I told him that I just knew he drank coffee since he was older than me. Both of my parents drank coffee, my grandparents drank coffee, and his parents drank coffee. Besides all that, I got the cutest little percolator for a gift at my bridal shower, and so that must mean that you drink coffee once you're married! Well then, Jim started laughing—not like a hyena, but pretty hard. So when he stopped laughing, he said to me, "You mean all these years we've been drinking coffee, it wasn't because you were already a coffee drinker, but because we received a percolator as a wedding gift?" To which I laughingly replied, "Pretty much!" I really enjoy my cup of coffee, even more now, because I think back to how Jim would drink it—not because he was a coffee drinker, but because he thought I was. I hope your day is filled with blessings. Go and make some happy memories with your loved ones!

I'm going to close with a couple of scriptures that I love.

So the Lord God cast a deep sleep on the man, and while he was asleep, he took out one of his ribs and closed up its place with flesh. The Lord God then built up into a woman the rib that he had taken from the man. When he brought her to the man, the man said: "This one, at last, is bone of my bones and flesh of my flesh; This one shall be called 'woman,' for out of 'her man' this one has been taken." That is why a man leaves his father and mother and clings to his wife, and the two of them become one body. (Genesis 2:21–24)

Love is patient; love is kind. Love is not jealous, it does not put on airs, it is not snobbish. Love is never rude, it is not self-seeking, it is not prone to anger; neither does it brood over injuries. Love does not rejoice in what is wrong but rejoices with the truth. There is no limit to love's forbearance, to its trust, its hope, its power to endure. (1 Corinthians 13:4–7)

Bye for now.
Sharla

A Cinnamon Stick, 40 Days, the Way, the Truth, and the Life

Friday, January 9, 2015

Hello out there! I hope y'all are having a good day. My last post was about my cute little percolator and the beginning of coffee in the mornings for Jim and me. The evening after I posted the story on my blog, Jim sat down and read it. We laughed again, and I asked him if he remembered the percolator. He said that he remembered it was small and cream colored. I replied, "Yes, and it had flowers painted on it." I told y'all in my post how we always drink Folgers Coffee. Well, that night when I prepared the coffee and set the delay brew button, I decided I wanted to add part of a cinnamon stick to the brew basket. The next morning, when I poured the coffee, I could smell the cinnamon. I thought it might be a nice change. I tasted the coffee and thought it tasted pretty good. Jim drank a cup, but he was not impressed. Needless to say, last night when I made the coffee, the cinnamon stick was left out. I can always sprinkle ground cinnamon in mine if I decide to try something different again!

I posted updated information on my 40 Days for Life Facebook page yesterday. I changed the cover picture. I replaced it with a picture I took of several of the brochures we have about abortion, adoption, healing after abortion, and help that is available at the pregnancy help centers. We offer the brochures in English and Spanish. We also have several prayer cards that are available. Take as many or as few as you like. Some people read them while they are at the prayer vigil for the unborn. I have to finish some paperwork for the family business, so I better close for now. I hope you all have a wonderful weekend!

"Jesus answered, 'I am the way and the truth and the life. No one comes to the Father except through me'" (John 14:6).

"Keep the light of Christ always shining in your hearts. Only He is the Way to be trodden. He is the Truth we must speak out. He is the Love we must love" (Mother Teresa).

Bye for now.
Sharla

More Babies Have to Die?

Thursday, January 22, 2015

Good morning out there! Today is the forty-second anniversary of Roe v. Wade. I woke up during the night to loud, booming thunder. I heard the rain pelt the windows, and as I listened, I thought how appropriate this storm seemed. Not a gentle peaceful rain, but a loud, hard rain. I could almost hear God say, "Why? What does it take? When will you wake up? How many more babies have to die? Isn't close to 58 million enough?" I stayed awake. I couldn't go back to sleep. I'm listening. I'm trying. Here I am, Lord.

Last week, I sent the local newspaper my blog post from December 4, 2014. I thought it would be a good article for today. I received an e-mail telling me that they couldn't print it in the section I asked for because the story was written as a poem. I understood, so I sent them a very short poem to be printed in the Letter to the Editor Opinion section. That one was apparently not appropriate either. I looked in today's newspaper, and they published an article about where trash cans should be located. Really? That is the best they could come up with for today? My heart is so heavy, and I'm sorry if you've already read these and were looking for something more today. But these posts are what my heart feels today. God bless you all.

Hello out there! My heart is sad today. I wish I knew what to say. I try to make others see, the gift of life a baby will be. Please,

God, show me the way, so that I can make a difference today. As tears stream down my face, I pray, Why does my heart ache this way? Please, God, give me the words. Please guide my hand as I write this verse. How do I make others see, the horrible death that abortion brings? Please, God, give me strength. Please give me courage to fight this fight that curses the earth.

Please, God, show me the way, that I can make a difference today.

Written by Sharla K. Ynostrosa

Coffee and a Road Trip for Life Part 1

Monday, January 26, 2015

Hello out there! I have so much to share with y'all, but I also have to go to the grocery store, so I will post part of my story today and the rest tomorrow! Guess where Jim and I were on Saturday? That's right! We were at the Texas Rally for Life in Austin, TX. The whole day was an amazing experience! It was such a huge blessing to be with so many pro-life people of all ages.

Our day began at 2:00 a.m., and that is not a typo; the alarm went off at 2:00 a.m.! Jim got up and went in the kitchen and poured coffee in our mugs and brought them back to the bedroom. I was still in bed thinking, "What in the world are we doing waking up at this time of night?" By the time I rolled out of bed, approximately 2:15 a.m., Jim was already dressed and telling me to get moving. After drinking about half a cup of coffee, I started waking up. By the time I finished that cup and started another, I was roaring to go! We left the house at 3:00 a.m. By this time, I was talking a mile a minute! Jim nicely reminded me that he was not quite as talkative as I was that early in the morning and to try and just enjoy the drive for a little bit! Well, that lasted all of ten minutes or so! Anyway, he drove to Mason, and then we switched, and I drove to some little place right outside of Austin, then Jim took over so I could navigate/pay attention to where we needed to go!

This was our schedule:

7:00 a.m. Met in front of Planned Parenthood on Ben White in Austin to pray the rosary with other pro-life Catholics.

9:15 a.m. The Living Rosary at St. Vincent de Paul Parish, Austin, TX. The children pantomimed the Joyful Mysteries and the students led the congregation in praying the Rosary for Life. The Dominican Sisters of Mary organized this beautiful Living Rosary. Absolutely precious, awesome, and heartwarming!

10:00 a.m. A pro-life Mass was celebrated, and the church was packed! We were shoulder to shoulder in the pews, and there were teenagers from parishes all across Texas standing all along the walls! My heart was so full, and still is, when I think about all the young people who are pro-life and proud of it!

I'll have to tell you about the march to the capitol and the Texas Rally for Life on the capitol steps and lawn tomorrow! Wonderful, amazing, incredible. So very, very thankful we were there!

I have to go to the store now. My dogs, Bella and Stormy, need food, and so do we! Y'all have a great day! I keep thinking about this Bible verse: "Seek and ye shall find" I so wanted and needed to see an abundance of other pro-life people, and what I witnessed on Saturday will stay in my heart for the rest of my life! Blessings to you and yours!

Bye for now.
Sharla

Coffee and a Road Trip for Life Part 2

Friday, January 30, 2015

Good morning out there! I know I told y'all that I would post the rest of my story about the Texas Rally for Life on Tuesday, and today is Friday, so I am three days late. I'm sorry! Life happens, and sometimes, things just don't go as planned! I hope you all have had a good week, and I'm sure that your week has been busy also! I stopped my story on Monday right before the part about the March for Life and the Rally! If you didn't read my post before this one and you have time, you might want to read it just to get the whole picture!

The Texas Rally for Life in Austin on Saturday, January 24, 2015, was an incredible experience. In my previous post, I told you how our day began praying the rosary at the Planned Parenthood on Ben White. Beginning the day this way really puts things in perspective. I mean, this is why we march. I can't adequately describe the feeling of standing in front of a fenced facility where abortions are performed. Just knowing that babies' lives are taken from them at that place leaves a sick feeling in your stomach. A surgery center is supposed to be a place of healing, a place to help you get better. When someone goes to an abortion facility, it isn't to get better. It is to pay an abortionist to end the life of their baby. It is a very sad and sobering experience.

Arriving at St. Vincent de Paul Church and seeing a packed parking lot was uplifting. Going into the sanctuary and seeing the young children pantomime the Joyful Mysteries of the Rosary while the older youth lead the prayers was a much-needed reminder of God's love and a visual image of the strong pro-life presence of families and people of all ages. As we sat shoulder to shoulder, stood side by side, kneeled right next to each other, with young adults from youth groups all across Texas standing along the walls, I was overcome with joy and peace and happiness, because together, with God, we are strong. A pro-life Mass was celebrated by Most Rev. Joe Vasquez, bishop of Austin. He gave a wonderful homily, and the entire Mass was beautiful. I remember kneeling and praying at the end of Mass thanking God for such an amazing morning.

Driving to get to the march took a little time, but we made it. We found a parking place pretty quick. I was so excited when I saw all the people parking and walking toward the gathering area for the march. We ended up toward the front. The Knights of Columbus led the March. It was awesome. There were pro-life people everywhere! I loved all the different pro-life T-shirts, the banners, the signs! I loved when we prayed the Mysteries of the Rosary, sang the Divine Mercy Chaplet, and when someone would holler out, "We are," and the rest of us would holler back, "Pro-Life!" It was great! Back to the signs. Several of the teenagers held signs that said, "My Generation Will End Abortion." Others held signs that said, "We are the Pro-Life Generation!" Many of the signs were handwritten on poster boards. One of these signs said, "1/3 of My Generation Is Missing." Another one said, "I Survived, but Roe v. Wade Won't Survive Me!" One of my favorites was, "'A person is a person no matter how small!' Dr. Seuss." We marched several blocks to get to the Capitol. The weather was perfect, and being with so many pro-life people of all ages, so many teenagers and young adults, was absolutely fantastic!

As we walked onto the Capitol lawn, pro-abortion protesters jumped out at us, yelling in our faces, waving their signs with crude statements. We just kept walking and totally ignored them. We stood in the shade of the trees and listened to the guest speakers for the rally. Each one had a story to tell. Abby Johnson was the emcee, and she shared a little of her story as she introduced each speaker. I don't have time to tell you about each speech, but I do want to at least tell you about one. Her name is Claire Culwell, and the story she told brought tears to my eyes. I listened as tears streamed down my face. She was adopted when she was about 2.5 months old. She was premature and only weighed a little over three pounds when she was born, and she had several problems that required casting for her little legs and lower body. She looked for her birth mother when she was older. She is in her mid- to late twenties now. The story her birth mother told her changed her life. Claire survived the abortion that killed her twin. I can't imagine hearing those words. Claire's story is one you should read about. If you go to the Texas Alliance for Life page and click on pictures from the Texas Rally for Life, you will see her beautiful picture, and you can read the rest of her story. When all the speakers were finished, we walked back to our vehicles. There were at least 2,500 pro-life people there. I've heard different numbers, even as high as 6,000. That wouldn't surprise me. There were people as far as I could see and then some.

Jim and I headed back to San Angelo, tired from waking up at 2:00 a.m., but energized from the wonderful experience the entire day had been. I was disappointed with the media coverage. The liberal media refused to acknowledge the huge pro-life presence that is growing stronger each year. The liberal media refused to acknowledge the young men and women who carry signs that say, "My Generation

Will End Abortion!" You know what? I believe their generation will end it! Thanks be to God!

"Ask, and you will receive. Seek, and you will find. Knock, and it will be opened to you. For the one who asks, receives. The one who seeks, finds. The one who knocks, enters" (Matthew 7:7–8).

Lead Me Lord, by the Light of Truth, to Seek and to Find the Narrow Way

Tuesday, February 10, 2015

Good morning out there! A quick post to say hello, and I hope you are all doing well! I woke up this morning with a whole list of things to do running through my mind. I'm trying to plan out my day so that I can accomplish all that needs to get done. I'm on my second cup of coffee, so that should help!

The 40 Days for Life Spring Campaign begins next week, starting on Ash Wednesday! I've been advertising on my Facebook page, and I have a Facebook page for the campaign: 40 Days for Life —San Angelo, TX (if you ever want to check out all the information or see the pictures that I post). I've also been calling people who participated in the fall campaign to see if they would like to sign up again. Most people are signing back up! We had a table in the vestibule at church this past weekend with sign-up sheets and flyers. I made a backdrop of pictures from the fall campaign and had it on the table. I went to Hobby Lobby on Friday and bought one of those cardboard tri-folds that you use for presentations at school. I downloaded a bunch of pictures that I took during the fall campaign and had them developed at Walgreens. I taped two informational flyers about the campaign, one in English and one in Spanish, on the middle section of the tri-fold. Then I cut out different shapes, colors, and sizes of colored poster board and taped them all over the tri-fold and then taped the pictures on there. It turned out really well. I wanted people to see all the different families, friends, and rosary groups that participated. The pictures showed children playing, sidewalk chalk pro-life messages and slogans, and smiling, happy faces! A picture is worth a thousand words! I can tell people all day long about the fellowship that happens during the 40 days, but the backdrop I made really shows it! Everyone enjoyed looking at the pictures, and several people signed up! I'll be on the phone again today, but not until I finish up some bookwork for our family business!

I better get busy. I just wanted to check in and say hello! I hope your day is full of blessings. The sun is shining here, so I'll open up the windows in a little while and let the fresh air in.

I'm going to close with a quote from Blessed Mother Teresa, "God has not called me to be successful. He has called me to be faithful."

Bye for now.
Sharla

Crazy Valentine's Day Commercials

Wednesday, February 11, 2015

Good morning out there! Just a quick post before I dash out the door! I just have to ask this, does anyone else think the "Hoodie-Footie" Valentine's Day commercial is goofy? I just can't imagine walking around my home in one of those outfits! I mean really? How in the world are you supposed to wash dishes, cook, do laundry, and all the other things that are necessary in something that a newborn or small baby wears? You certainly aren't going to take out the trash or throw scraps to the chickens in that getup! If you are that cold, turn up the thermostat or go scrub the tub; either one will warm you right up! Anyway, I just had to get that out!

If you are going to buy me something, I like chocolate! No, I don't need it, but I sure like it. Oh, don't buy me one of those four-foot teddy bears either. Where in the world are you going to keep that thing?

Thanks for letting me vent! Those commercials drive me crazy! I hope y'all have a super great day! Give your spouse a kiss, tell them, "Happy Valentine's Day," turn some music on, twirl around the kitchen while you're cooking, and hug your kids! And most importantly, thank God for a new day!

Bye for now.
Sharla

Please, God, Give Me the Words Guide My Hand as I Write This Verse

Thursday, February 12, 2015

Hello out there! I hope you all are having a great week! The spring 40 Days for Life Campaign starts next week! I am busy trying to tie up all the loose ends! Having said that, I have to share my nervous feelings about everything falling into place. Signing up to be the coordinator for the San Angelo 40 Days for Life Campaign helps keep my focus on what I want to do, what I believe in with all of my heart. But in all honesty, I'm not an in-charge type of person. I'd much rather someone else say, "This is what I want you to do," but for some reason, I am the coordinator. I pray for guidance, strength, and wisdom daily to do the very best I can to bring awareness about the help that is available for young ladies and women in a crisis pregnancy. I pray for ways to bring more people out to pray for an end to abortion, because I know that with prayer, all things are possible! The following prayer is one that we pray daily during the 40 Days for Life:

> Lord God, I thank you today for the gift of
> my life and for the lives of all my brothers and
> sisters. I know there is nothing that destroys

more life than abortion, yet I rejoice that you have conquered death by the resurrection of Your Son. I am ready to do my part in ending abortion.

Today, I commit myself never to be silent, never to be passive, never to be forgetful of the unborn. I commit myself to be active in the Pro-Life Movement and never to stop defending life until all my brothers and sisters are protected and our nation once again becomes a nation with liberty and justice, not just for some, but for all. Through Christ, our Lord. Amen.

I love this prayer, and I'm going to highlight how I pray that God will help me to live my life every day, not just during the 40 Days for Life campaigns.

"Today, I commit myself never to be silent, never to be passive, never to be forgetful of the unborn. I commit myself to be active in the Pro-Life Movement and never to stop defending life until all my brothers and sisters are protected and our nation once again becomes a nation with liberty and justice, not just for some, but for all."

Please pray for me and all the coordinators and participants of the 40 Days for Life campaigns. Please pray that God will guide us, give us strength, courage, and perseverance, and please pray for our families. Thank you.

Bye for now.
Sharla

A Quiet Moment in the Courtyard, Listening to God

Friday, February 27, 2015

Brrrrrr...It's cold this morning! Hello out there! The roads are icy this morning, so we will have a late start at the courtyard! Since I don't have to head out so early, I want to share what has been happening at our 40 Days vigil.

On Tuesday, my husband attached tarps on two sides of one of the canopies we have out at the courtyard. That really helped to block the wind that day. He also lit two small propane heaters and sat them in front of the open side. We sat chairs inside and put some blankets in there. We hung up all the pro-life signs, and he headed off to work. I really didn't think many people would come and pray because it was so cold. I was wrong. People who were signed up for certain hours showed up to pray. People just dropped in to pray. There is no way to describe how thankful I am for these devoted pro-life warriors! The sun came out for a little while in the afternoon, and some people sat outside of the warming area, all bundled up and prayed.

Wednesday morning, I was ready to go! I arrived at the courtyard at 7:00 a.m. and started setting the chairs out and hanging up the pictures and posters that we take down at night. I put a clean sign-up sheet on the clipboard and made sure that the daily devotional page from 40 Days was in the prayer books. One of my dearest friends, Candi, stopped by to help me set up. She stayed for a while and then told me she would be back so that I could go home. It was a beautiful morning. The sun was shining, and there were little ladybugs all over the posters and the planters. I was so happy to be outside and enjoy the sunshine. I prayed, and I sang the Divine Mercy Chaplet. Candi came back and sent me home. I told her that I would be back so that she could go to the noon Mass. It was such a beautiful day. I just knew that lots and lots of people would be stopping by to pray! People did come, one at a time at first, and then two or three. A young man who attends college came at his regular time. Two ladies who have been praying during the 40 Days for years came and prayed. I left for a little while during this time, and when I returned, Candi was there. She and I were the only ones left, and she helped me get some pro-life brochures together to take to St Mary's youth later on that evening. I think it was about 4:15 or so when she was leaving. She has been such a blessing to me, such a wonderful friend, always seems to know just when I need her to stop by. After she left, I sat down at the picnic table underneath the oak trees. I prayed and told God that I thought there would be more people that day. I sat there quietly and prayed. It was so peaceful. I heard a noise and looked up to see two squirrels chasing each other up and down the oak tree. I smiled at their playfulness. One squirrel ran off, and the other one came closer to me. I looked down at him and said, "Are you here to pray with me today?" I heard a bird singing in the tree above me. I looked up, and birds were flying in and out of the trees. Something caught my eye, and I glanced over and saw that same little squirrel sitting on the fence that surrounds the courtyard. He was sitting up straight, his little paws together and his headed tilted upward. His little mouth was moving, and I laughingly exclaimed, "You are praying with me!" I thanked God for the quiet, peaceful moments. I felt like God was reminding me that I am never alone, He is always with me. So I sat there and prayed, thanking God for this quiet time I had alone with Him in the peaceful courtyard, where birds sing, squirrels play, ladybugs fly, and people come and pray. A few moments later, people started arriving. One sat here, and one sat there. Hugs and prayers, fellowship everywhere.

What happened that day will forever stay in my heart, a reminder from God to be still and know that He is always with me. God is always with you. Be still and quiet and listen. Stay warm and be safe. If the roads are icy, stay at home and pray! Blessings to you and yours!

Bye for now.
Sharla

Winter Weather Blessings from the Courtyard

Sunday, March 1, 2015

Hello out there! Today is day 12 of the 40 Days for Life campaign. We did not pray at the courtyard on day 10 and day 11 because the roads were icy, and it was too dangerous to get out! I told everyone to stay safe and pray from wherever they were at. Yesterday afternoon, Jim and I drove to the courtyard and checked out the ice situation. The concrete was iced over below the oak trees and as you walk in through the gates. So we devised a plan of action for this morning.

Step 1: Get out of bed at 5:15 a.m. Jim did. I didn't.

Step 2: Make the coffee because we didn't last night. Jim did. I didn't.

Step 3: Get dressed and ready to go. Jim was. I wasn't.

At 5:45 a.m. or so, I finally got up. Jim brought me some coffee to drink while I was getting ready. He went and loaded up two push brooms, a regular broom, rock salt, and Epsom salt (because we didn't have enough rock salt) and started the truck and turned on the heater so that it could warm up. He also warmed up some tortillas and heated up some bacon I had cooked yesterday and made us a bacon tortilla wrap for breakfast (yummy)! Yes, I know. I am very blessed to have such a wonderful husband. I thank God for him all the time. We are a team. We work together. After two cups of coffee, I was ready to go! We loaded up and head to the courtyard. It was dark and a light mist was falling. The trees were covered in ice and look so pretty and shimmery (not sure if that is a word or not, but I like it)!

We got to the courtyard and carefully walked through the gate. I started sprinkling salt, and Jim started pushing the broom. I went and got a big trash can out for the leaves and a stand-up dust pan. Another vehicle pulled up, and our friend Doug stepped out. He was there to pray, but he set up the chairs and grabbed a broom to help Jim first. It was cold, but the wind wasn't blowing so it was not too bad. We set up the propane heaters and lit one. After the work was done, we sat down to pray. About 9:30 a.m., Muriel showed up. She was dressed up ready to go to the 10:00 a.m. Mass, but she sat down to pray for a little while first. Right before 10:00, Muriel head to Mass, and at 10:00, Doug head home. I asked Jim if he would please go and get me some coffee from McDonalds and maybe some oatmeal too! I felt like I had burned off the bacon tortilla wrap already. (Probably not, but I like to think so!) Jim took off, and I was in the courtyard by myself, and I just sat by the little heater and read from my daily devotional book. I watched the ice fall from the trees as it began to melt, and I just felt so at peace.

Jim got back and I went and sat in the truck with him while I ate my oatmeal, and he ate some kind of McMuffin thing. Then we went back into the courtyard and sat down and started reading our devotional. Mass ended, and Rickie and Irma stopped by to say hello. Irma said that she and her mama would probably be back to pray later on. Muriel showed up and told us to go home. She sent me a picture about an hour ago of her legs wrapped in a blanket and red cotton gloves on her feet propped up by the heater. The caption read something like, "Keeping my toes toasty warm!" She is so funny and so devoted. She told me that Phyllis was there and that she was leaving and Matt will be there from 1:00 p.m. to 2:00 p.m.

Muriel was going to go back at 2:00 p.m. and stay until Jim and I went back at 3:00 p.m. We went to the 6:00 p.m. Mass so someone will take our place while we were at Mass. Praying hours in the court-yard are from 7:00 a.m. to 7:00 p.m.

Tomorrow will be another day full of blessings. Come and join us if you can. If not, please pray from wherever you are! The babies and their families need our prayers!

I'm going to close with the following scripture: "We are the clay, and you are our potter; we are all the work of your hand" (Isaiah 64:8).

Bye for now.

Sharla

Blessing 9: Camping Out at Nana and Pa's Home, and Praying the Rosary

Tuesday, March 10, 2015

Good morning out there! Joyful news! Grandchild number 9 was born this past weekend, a healthy baby girl! Her four siblings are camping out at Pa and Nana's home (Jim and I) for a couple of days! I haven't been able to get out to the courtyard very much the last couple of days because I have been cooking for four extra hungry mouths, washing dishes, washing hair, brushing hair, wiping mouths, and changing diapers. I've also been washing lots of clothes! But the best part is, I've also received lots of hugs, lots of kisses, heard lots of mealtime and bedtime prayers, and heard the words, "I love you, Nana," so I feel very blessed! I have to close now. I'm needed in the kitchen. It is time to cook breakfast for my little chickadees!

Bye for now.
Sharla

As a Catholic, I pray the Sorrowful Mysteries of the Rosary on Tuesdays and Fridays. I am going to change things up a bit today and pray the Joyful Mysteries instead. My heart is full of joy!

Signs Are Everywhere, Just Open Your Eyes, Listen to Your Heart!

Thursday, March 19, 2015

Good morning out there! Today is day 30 of the 40 Days for Life Campaign. A quick post before I head to the courtyard. I have been blessed in so many ways during the campaign. I will post a summary of the campaign at a later date, but I wanted to share what happened last night.

I didn't get to the courtyard until 6:00 p.m. last night because I had to take my granddaughters, who live out of town to meet their other grandmother. The drive is about two and a half hours one way. We had a busy morning. My daughter and her two girls stopped by with donuts so that "the cousins" could see each other for a little while before we left. While they played, Jess and I finished packing up for the girls. They left, and we loaded up and headed to see my daughter-in-law and the rest of the cousins, including our newest blessing, a baby girl born last week. They live about thirty-five miles from us. We arrived at their home. They held the baby and then dashed off to play with their older cousins. I held one of the younger granddaughters on my lap while my daughter-in-law fed the baby, and we had a nice visit. Her stepmother, a wonderful lady, was there also. I rounded up the kids, gave them all a kiss, and my other two granddaughters and I headed off on our journey. We stopped to pick up some lunch, sang silly songs, and talked about all kinds of things. We arrived at our destination, unloaded their bags from my truck, and loaded them up in their other grandmother's vehicle, and then hugs, kisses, and good-byes were said. I received a phone call while we were on the road. It was from a sweet lady who also goes to Sacred Heart. She said that she had a gift for me and that she and her husband wanted to stop by the courtyard and give it to me. I explained about the road trip and told her that I would be at the courtyard about 6:00 p.m. I prayed on the way home from the trip. I prayed about 40 Days for Life, my role as the coordinator in San Angelo, and asked what I needed to do to get more people involved. I told God how I felt, how much the pro-life movement meant to me. I told Him how much I wanted to get the message out, but sometimes, I wondered if I was headed in the right direction. I felt at peace after I prayed because I knew He would lead me. I knew I just needed to listen. I sang this refrain as I closed my prayer: "Lead me, Lord. Lead me, Lord, by the light of truth, to seek and to find the narrow way. Be my way. Be my truth. Be my life, my Lord, and lead me, Lord. Lead me, Lord. Lead me, Lord, today."

I arrived at the courtyard at 6:00 p.m., and the couple from church pulled up at the same time. We laughed when we got out of our vehicles at the good timing. She held a beautiful bag covered with red roses and tissue paper in her hand. We walked over to the picnic table in the courtyard and sat down. I told her how sweet it was of her to bring me a gift. She wanted to explain why she bought the gift. She told me that our Blessed Mother wanted me to have this. I felt my chest get tight and reached inside the bag and pulled the box out carefully. When I opened it, tears welled in my eyes. There was the most beautiful two-sided plaque. On the left side was a picture of Our Lady of Guadalupe, the one picture that shows our Blessed Mother pregnant with our Lord.

The following prayer is on the right hand side of the plaque:

> Our Lady of Guadalupe, Mother of Life, cast your maternal gaze on your children, born and unborn. We are in such need of your protection. The enemies of life are strong, but you are infinitely stronger, since God chose you to "crush the head of the serpent," the devil. As we strive to overcome evil we remember your words of comfort to St. Juan Diego, "Am I not here, who am your mother?! Therefore, we approach you with great confidence.
>
> Our Lady of Guadalupe, Mother of Life, Pray for Us!

She then told me that they received all kinds of catalogs, and she usually just threw them away, but for some reason, she kept this one. She looked through the catalog and saw the picture of this plaque and thought, "Oh, I bet Sharla would love this!" Then she thought, "She probably already has one." She didn't throw the catalog away, and she kept going back to the picture, and she felt like she was supposed to buy it for me. I wish I could describe the emotion that went through me. I thought about my prayer earlier. They had no idea what the timing of this gift meant to me. I thanked them profusely, and about that time, two people, a faithful mom and her teenage son, came to pray. I showed them the gift. We visited for a little while longer, and then they left. I sat down to pray. As I prayed, I watched my little squirrel dash to and fro and the birds fly in and out of the trees. The noise from the traffic seemed to be at a distance as I prayed and thanked God for letting me know that I needed to press on. I thought I was going to write a quick post, but God had other plans. I really must get to the courtyard now. I pray that your day is full of blessings.

Bye for now.
Sharla

The Courtyard
A Place Where You Are
Always Welcome

Saturday, March 21, 2015

Hello out there! The month of March has been full of life for our family. The spring 40 Days for Life campaign has been going on, and we have been blessed with the birth of grandchild number 9 and are expecting the birth of grandchild number 10 sometime next week. The girls outnumber the boys four to one! Yes, we are very blessed to be the grandparents of ten (this includes our granddaughter who is due to make her appearance next week) healthy, happy, full of life and energy grandchildren.

I spent Tuesday with my daughter and her three daughters, including the little one who is due next week. We were also accompanied by three more of my granddaughters, those old enough to enjoy lunch and a movie. We took them to see Cinderella, and it was a really good movie. I'm so thankful that I was able to spend the day with so many of my girls! My mom died of cancer when I was twelve, so I really treasure the relationship I have with my daughter. I love spending time with all of my grandchildren, but Tuesday was just for girls. Life is amazing, two new babies born within a couple of weeks of each other. Two baby girls growing up together as cousins and friends.

Today is day 32 of the 40 Days for Life Campaign. I wanted to share something that I realized on Thursday.

Even though we are not in front of an abortion facility, people come through the gates of the courtyard for many reasons. Some come to talk, some just need a listening ear, and some tell us that they pray as they pass the signs and banners. One young man came in through the gates asking, "Is this where we pray about abortion?" It was a very cold morning, and we invited him to sit down by the heater and pray with us. He sat down, and we gave him a blanket to cover up with, and he prayed with us for a while, thanked us, and as he started to leave, I asked him if he knew about the Sack Lunch Ministry. His name is Michael, and he replied that he didn't. So as the other ladies continued to pray, I walked with him to the back of the kitchen and showed him where they handed out the lunches and told him the times. I reached out my hand to shake his as I said good-bye, but instead of shaking my hand, he hugged me and said, "God bless you," and then he went on his way. Some people take brochures with them, and many stay and visit a while after they have prayed. The fellowship we all share is wonderful.

We've told people about the Sack Lunch Ministry and handed out waters. It is amazing what happens when you are just there, out in the open, a smile on your face, saying, "Come on in. We are here for you."

So as you go about your day, hold your head high, make eye contact with people, and smile.

A smile goes a long way. And if you are out and about in San Angelo, come join us in the courtyard at Sacred Heart, a place where you are always welcome.

Bye for now.
Sharla

A Rainy Day, Church Bells and Blessing 10

Wednesday, April 1, 2015

Good morning out there! Perfect spring weather! The sun is shining, and there is a cool breeze in the air! I opened up the windows to let the fresh air in. I hope you all are having a wonderful week. This is Holy Week, a week full of blessings and miracles and mercy and love. I have so much to share with all of you. Blessing number 10, another grandchild, another sweet baby girl, was born last week! March was full of blessings for our family. Two baby girls were born just a couple of weeks apart! Two more granddaughters for us to love!

Let me tell you about the Saturday before blessing number 10 arrived.

It was a rainy day, kind of gloomy. The morning was cold. I headed to the courtyard (40 Days for Life was still going on) about 7:00 a.m. I arrived, and two people were praying. I unlocked the door to the hallway, and a sweet lady came inside to pray while the nice man stayed outside beneath the canopy to pray. I organized the prayer books and put out a new sign-up sheet. I read my daily devotionals and waited for the next person to arrive. My friend and fellow prayer warrior arrived, and after a hug and a quick visit, I drove home and started cooking a pot of beans that I had let soak overnight. My daughter called and asked if I was still at the courtyard. When I told her that no, I was home, she told me that she and the girls were coming over. While I waited, I added seasoning to the beans and grated cheese for quesadillas. The girls arrived about noon. They were ready to eat! After lunch and some playtime, we all settled down to rest for a bit. My oldest granddaughter was resting on the couch, covered up with a patchwork quilt my grandmother had made. My daughter was asleep on the smaller couch, her hand resting protectively over her stomach with blessing number 10 still nestled snug inside. I sat in the rocking chair holding my younger granddaughter, rocking back and forth. I quietly sang the "Hail Mary" until my granddaughter fell asleep. As I sat there, rocking back and forth, I felt so at peace. I thought about how blessed I am to have been adopted at birth and to be able to share this Saturday afternoon with my daughter and three of my granddaughters. The lights were out, and the room was cool. All my girls were sound asleep. I could smell the aroma of simmering beans in the air. I thought about my husband and son, who were working on the bells up in the bell tower at St. Boniface, and said a prayer. It went something like this, "Dear Lord, please don't let them fall through the floor, down the stairs, or out of the windows. They are doing this out of the goodness of their hearts and because they love you so much, so please keep them safe. Amen." I rocked some more, holding my little one close, and prayed again, "Dear God, thank you for my blessings, my husband, my sons and their wives, and their children, my grandchildren. Thank you for my daughter, her husband, and their children, my grandchildren. Thank you for the gift of our lives. Thank you for this quiet moment. I love you so very much. Amen." After a little while, the girls woke up, and they headed back to their home. My husband arrived safely, and I asked him about being in the bell tower. He said something like, "Piece of cake," and then grinned, because it wasn't! But that's him. He doesn't complain. He just does what needs to be done, and that is just one of the many reasons I love him so much! He also told me that they were having Eucharistic Adoration at the same time they were up in the bell tower. I just thought, "How awesome is that?" He said they probably prayed harder when they heard all the metal banging above their heads going on, and I laughed! I told him that I hoped no "ugly" words were said, and he replied that no cussing had taken place, but there may have been some raised voices, to which I raised my eyebrows and kind of grinned! I asked if he wanted to ride with me to close up the courtyard, and he said, "Not really," but he went with me anyway. The next day, we both spent a lot of time at the courtyard, praying for the babies, praying for their mothers and their fathers. We prayed for families everywhere, and we thanked God for our many blessings. The 40 Days for Life campaign ended on Palm Sunday. Please continue to pray for the unborn and their families. They need our prayers. I'm going to close with something I wrote last summer.

Gifts from heaven, Babies are
Gifts from God above
Protect them, Love them
Sing songs of joy
New life, New life
How precious they are!
Written by Sharla K. Ynostrosa

I'll Say a Little Prayer for You!

Friday, April 17, 2015

Good morning out there! I have so much to say. Where do I begin? I'll start off with what an absolutely beautiful morning it is. I walked my husband out to his truck as he was heading to work. I smiled at him as he rolled down his window, and I sang, "I'll say a little prayer for you!" I watched him back out of the driveway, and I blew him a kiss good-bye.

I wish I could say that I do that every morning. I should do that every morning, but I don't. This morning was different. Where do I begin?

As I've told you in my previous posts, we are self-employed. My husband is a contract welder, and I keep the books. We've been married for almost thirty-two years now, and we've been self-employed for the last twenty-five years. Needless to say, we've seen many ups and downs in our business, but by the grace of God, we are still in business. Feast or famine, boom or bust, yep that is the oil field. Now that we are older and our children are grown, we can handle the ups and downs a lot easier. Thanks be to God, our home is paid off. Jim worries about the other guys and their families. He feels bad for those whose homes are not paid off, for those who have babies on the way. I feel his pain too. We have been there, so we know what they are going through.

I made the coffee last night and set the automatic timer so that it would be ready when we woke up. I got up when Jim did, and I went to the kitchen and started cooking bacon. I saw the box of Graham Crackers on the countertop and smiled. Jim has a sweet tooth, and the chocolate chip cookies I made earlier in the week are all gone! I sat down at the kitchen counter and started filling out invoices for the work that Jim has done the last couple of weeks. He came in the kitchen, and we checked everything over. Today might be the last day he contracts for this company. Hours have been cut, and there is not much to do. We know the drill; contractors are usually the first to go.

We reminisced about a similar Friday many years ago. On that Friday, Jim was not self-employed; he was an employee and had been for about eight years. I was 8 1/2 months pregnant with our son when Jim came home early that day. I was busy putting away baby things that I had received at my baby shower just the night before. I was surprised when I heard Jim come through the door. I'll never forget the look on his face, the disbelief, the hurt. He explained that he had been let go, and so had many others. It was hard, and we struggled, but we made it through. We learned to really depend on God, and we clung together as husband and wife, and our relationship has only grown stronger through the ups and downs.

Today is a new day. I don't know what is in store for today. I don't know if Jim will walk through the door early or if he will come home at the regular time. What I do know is we will be okay. God will see us through. We will lean on Him; we have learned that through the years, and we are stronger because of that. Our faith has made us stronger. I pray for those who have not yet learned to lean on God. I pray that their struggles will strengthen their relationships with each other and with God. I'm going to make some brownies for Jim today. I'll make sure they have pecans in them because those are his favorite. The brownies will be waiting on the counter for him, whether he comes home early or at the regular time; and I'll be here waiting for him, just like I always have.

I hope your day is full of blessings. Please pray for people everywhere. Our prayers do so much good. God is always listening. Pray for young couples. Pray for all couples and families to learn to cling to each other and to God. I'm going to close with this scripture:

"May the God of hope fill you with all joy and peace as you trust in Him" (Romans 15:13).

Hymns of Praise, Joyful Mysteries, and Pro-Life Banners

Thursday, April 30, 2015

Good morning out there! The sun is shining, the birds are singing, and there is a slight nip in the air! A gorgeous Thursday morning! I opened the curtains to let the sun shine in and raised the windows to let the cool morning air in! I'm going to go and fill up my coffee mug, and then I will visit with y'all! Okay, I am ready to get started! I warmed up my coffee and grabbed a big red delicious apple. I really wanted a big fat muffin or something similar, but I'm trying to eat healthier, for today anyway!

The other day, I was telling y'all about the banners I ordered. I'm very blessed to have so many friends and fellow pro-life warriors who support spreading the pro-life message. I'm very thankful for those who pitched in to help with the cost of the banners. Thank you. Thank you from the bottom of my heart!

I decided that Tuesday evening would be a good time to get together and hang up the banners and pray the pro-life rosary. So on Monday, I started calling people and letting them know about my plans. I also posted the time and date on Facebook. Little did I know that Tuesday would end up being a chilly, overcast day! I wondered if I should change the day and decided that no, the banners would go up and those who showed up would pray with me and it would just be okay!

I loaded my truck up with all the banners, prayer books, and handouts. I headed to the courtyard, and right when I pulled up, people started arriving! My smile was so big. My heart was so full. Our music minister/choir director came with his wife, and he sang three beautiful songs while we hung up two of the banners. I'm so thankful for him and how he shares his beautiful gift. He had picked out the perfect songs, and I was not the only one with tears in my eyes. He headed off to choir practice, and some more people arrived. We started praying the Joyful Mysteries of the Pro-Life Rosary. We usually pray the Sorrowful Mysteries on Tuesday, but the Joyful Mysteries seemed appropriate for the event and also because my heart was so full of joy! People took turns reading each mystery as we prayed. I'm going to post the Joyful Mysteries so that you can see what I'm talking about if you have never prayed the rosary before.

First Joyful Mystery
The Annunciation

"And when the angel had come to her, he said, 'Hail, full of grace, the Lord is with thee. Blessed art thou among women'" (Luke 1:28).

(When we pray the pro-life rosary, we add special intentions after each mystery/scripture.)

Mary is troubled by the angel's greeting yet rejoices to do God's will. Let us pray that those who are troubled by their pregnancy may have the grace to trust in God's will.

Second Joyful Mystery
The Visitation

"Elizabeth was filled with the Holy Spirit and cried out in a loud voice: 'Blest are you among women and blest is the fruit of your womb'" (Luke 1:41–42). John the Baptist leapt for joy in his mother's womb. We pray that people may realize that abortion is not about children who *might* come into the world but is about children who are already in the world, living and growing in the womb and are scheduled to be killed.

Third Joyful Mystery
The Birth of Jesus

"She gave birth to her first-born Son and wrapped Him in swaddling clothes and laid Him in a manger, because there was no room for them in the place where travelers lodged" (Luke 2:7).

God Himself was born as a child. The greatness of a person does not depend on size for the newborn King is very small. Let us pray for an end to prejudice against the tiny babies threatened by abortion.

Fourth Joyful Mystery
The Presentation

"When the day came to purify them according to the law of Moses, the couple brought Him up to Jerusalem so that He could be presented to the Lord, for it is written in the law of the Lord, 'Every first-born male shall be consecrated to the Lord'" (Luke 2:22–23). The Child is presented in the temple because the Child belongs to God. Children are not the property of their parents nor of the government. They, and we, belong to God Himself.

Fifth Joyful Mystery
Finding the Child Jesus in the Temple

"On the third day they came upon Him in the temple sitting in the midst of the teachers, listening to them and asking them questions" (Luke 2:46).

The boy Jesus was filled with wisdom because He is God. Let us pray that all people may see the wisdom of His teachings about the dignity of life and may understand that this teaching is not an opinion but the truth.

After each intention, we pray one Our Father, ten Hail Marys, one Glory be to the Father, and one Oh, My Jesus prayer. For the Pro-Life Rosary, we add, "Jesus, protect and save the unborn" at the end before starting the next mystery.

Now back to my story. It was wonderful! Praying together is such a powerful witness, so uplifting, so necessary! We looked at all the banners, and everyone agreed that each one was perfect! We will rotate them out every couple of weeks or so. That way, people will see a variety of beautiful, positive, thought-provoking pro-life messages as they drive or walk by the courtyard! We visited for a while, and then people helped roll up the other banners, and we loaded everything back into my truck. Overall, I counted right at thirty people, including the kids who came out to the courtyard to see the banners and pray on that chilly evening. I just want you to know what a blessing that hour in the courtyard was for me. The fellowship, the music, the prayers, and the wonderful feeling that God was right there with us, help keep me motivated to keep up the good fight! There are many days when I pray and ask God to guide me in how to spread the pro-life message, if I need to do something else. Then I spend an hour with y'all in the courtyard, and I know that He is telling me to stay the course, continue on this path, and don't ever give up!

Blessings! Blessings to you and yours! Please say a little prayer for me on this journey, and be assured that I will always be praying for each of you!

I am going to close with this scripture: "Welcome one another, then, as Christ welcomed you" (Romans 15:7).

Bye for now.
Sharla

Prayer Is the Answer

Friday, May 1, 2015

Good morning out there! Just a quick post to say hello, and I hope your day goes well. I woke up this morning with my grandchildren on my mind. I read the newspaper last night, and that was probably not a good idea. I know that I can't hide my head in the sand, but there are just so many horrible things in this old world. It just breaks my heart. So last night and this morning, I did the best thing I could do, I prayed. I talked to God and told him my fears and my worries. I lifted up my family in prayer. I lifted up friends and the special intentions that I've been asked to pray about. Last night, when Jim and I prayed before eating dinner, we gave thanks for our meal and then prayed for the sick. After I named off everyone I knew who needed and had asked for our prayers, Jim started naming those I had forgotten to mention. I love that we pray together. I'm so thankful that we remind each other about all those who need our prayers. When someone asks us to pray for them, we really take it to heart. This morning, when Jim was leaving for work, he reminded me about someone else we needed to pray for. I thank God for blessing me with such a wonderful husband. He is an awesome example for our children and grandchildren.

Bye for now.
Sharla

God, Peanut Butter, and a Good Marriage!

Tuesday, May 12, 2015

Good morning out there! I hope your Tuesday morning is starting off well! It is cloudy and cool outside this morning. It rained sometime during the night, and we have a pretty good chance for more rain this morning. I'm always thankful for the rain!

Jim has already headed off to work. We are both thankful that he is still working, and we are praying for those who have been let go. Life is full of ups and downs, the good and the bad, the happy and the sad. The other day, I was listening to the local Catholic radio station as I was running errands, and I heard the neatest thing. I caught the end of the program, but it was about how to have a happy and long marriage, you know, the "death until you part" kind of marriage. A married couple is the hosts for this particular program, and their guest was a priest. He gave one of the best analogies I've ever heard about how a couple must have God in their lives. He said that a husband and wife are like two pieces of bread and if you just place them together, they will fall apart. But if you put peanut butter on the bread and then place them together, the two pieces of bread will stick together. God is the peanut butter that holds the couple together! Don't you just love that? I laughed and laughed. I couldn't wait to tell Jim. Well, he also thought it was a great way to describe how we need God in our lives.

This morning, I fixed Jim some peanut-butter-and-jelly crackers. While I was in the kitchen, Jim was in our room getting ready for work. As I put the peanut butter on the crackers, I thought about what that priest said. I poured a cup of coffee for Jim and carried it to our room. He was kneeling on our hard floor saying his morning prayers. I sat the coffee down on the dresser, placed my hand on his shoulder, and kissed the top of his head. An overwhelming feeling came over me. I just felt so blessed that in our marriage, we have God to help hold us together.

May your day be full of blessings.

Bye for now.
Sharla

Thankful for God's Blessings

Tuesday, June 2, 2015

Hello out there! How are y'all doing? I haven't posted anything new in almost three weeks! It isn't that I haven't had anything to say or to share with y'all; I have just been so busy! Here is a condensed version, a kind of quick summary.

My life is full of busy blessings! When you have ten grandchildren, there is always some place to go, something to see, and fun things to do! So here are a few of my activities the past three weeks.

We have been entertained and enjoyed being at the following productions: tap and jazz recital, pre-K graduation, parish family picnic, Little League game, birthday party for one of our granddaughters who turned nine, and Memorial Day weekend with all our children and grandchildren combined. Third grade awards ceremony, Baskin Robbins for ice cream, feeding hungry tummies, and putting Band-Aids on wounded knees and toes! Kissing all the boo-boos, nap time, and rocking back and forth. Spending time with our grandchildren and adult children is the best! I love watching all the kids play together. The age ranges are two baby granddaughters, eight weeks and eleven weeks old; two toddler granddaughters, almost two years and three years old; one pre-K graduate grandson who is almost five; two young granddaughters, six and a half and almost eight years old; and three nine-year-olds, our oldest grandchild, who is also our oldest grandson, and our two oldest granddaughters, born just over two months apart! Blessings and blessings galore!

Now I will share what has been going on with church activities. I mentioned the parish family picnic above. It was held at the city park, and there were about 250 people who came and enjoyed spending time with family and friends. Both of our parish priests were at the picnic having a good time! We served chili dogs, chips, desserts, and drinks! The junior high and high school kids were playing touch football and basketball. The younger kids were playing tug-o-war and other games. The young kids were swinging and sliding and climbing! Parents were playing with their children, and it was awesome! I also noticed that the older teenagers were too busy having fun to be talking on the phone or texting! I loved seeing their smiling faces and listening to them laugh. It was just a great evening!

The next event is something very near and dear to my heart, and that is trying to spread the pro-life message on a daily basis! I had a lot of help planning this get-together, and I am so thankful for everyone involved! I especially want to thank my husband for fabricating the frames for our pro-life banners! About 40 people gathered in the courtyard at Sacred Heart to pray the Pro-Life Rosary after we hung up the banner of Our Lady of Guadalupe. A beautiful picture of Our Lady of Guadalupe and the statement "God Is Pro-Life. Are You?" is what the banner says. We took turns leading each decade of the rosary. We prayed two decades in Spanish and three decades in English.

I love praying the rosary. We prayed the Joyful Mysteries. They are so beautiful. After we prayed the rosary and closing prayer, we gathered in the cafeteria and all enjoyed a potluck dinner. We had plenty of food, and we invited other groups who were at the church for other meetings to join us. The cafeteria was full! The Life Teen group joined us also. Many of them prayed the rosary with us! It was an evening of blessings for me! Helping with our parish Sack Lunch

Ministry is something else near and dear to me. I am so thankful for this wonderful ministry that feeds so many. We provide sack lunches Monday through Friday from 11:00 a.m. to 1:00 p.m. I am only able to help two to three times a month right now, but I wish I could help every day. It is a wonderful ministry. We have been handing out over a hundred sack lunches a day! The sacks have words of encouragement and Bible verses on them. Sometimes the kids draw pictures on them for us. My heart is always so full after I help with this ministry.

This past weekend, I helped serve at the reception after the ordination of three priests! My eyes filled with tears as I watched the young priest greet the people and pray with those who came up for a blessing! These young men are all amazing. Their prayers are so heartfelt.

The night before the ordination, I woke up at about 2:30 a.m. It was raining outside, and as I lay there listening to the rain, I prayed for each of my grandchildren, and I prayed for the young men who would be ordained later on that morning. I thanked God that these young men said yes to devoting their lives to Him. I prayed that God would guide them and keep them safe and help them to always be discerning. It is so important that we pray for all our priests, bishops, deacons, the pope, and so on.

I hope I haven't bored you with my daily activities. I was just trying to catch up. I will try not to wait so long before my next post!

I hope your day is full of blessings, full of life, full of happiness. Whatever is going on in your life, remember to pray. God loves us all so much! Blessings to you and yours!

Bye for now.
Sharla

A Vacation, A Pilgrimage, Life and Healing

Friday, June 12, 2015

Hello out there! How are y'all doing? I am just fine! Jim and I returned home on Wednesday evening. We took a little vacation to celebrate our thirty-second wedding anniversary! We love to visit Catholic churches while we are on the road traveling from one place to the next. I like to think of it as a mini pilgrimage! I got out my big ole *Random House College Dictionary* to look up the complete definition of the word *pilgrimage*. On page 1006, it says, "pilgrimage n. 1. a journey, esp. a long one, made to some sacred place as an act of devotion. 2. any long journey, esp. one undertaken for a particular purpose, as to pay homage."

I'm not sure if our visits are really a pilgrimage, but they are definitely a must on any of our trips out of town. I don't know if Jim and I will ever make it to the Holy Land, Lourdes, Fatima, or to Rome, but we do try to visit Catholic churches wherever we travel! I'm going to start with some of the churches we visited on this trip. Before we head out of town, I look up the Catholic churches along our route and in the town or city we will be staying.

Last Friday, we went to the Cathedral Shrine of the Virgin of Guadalupe in Dallas, TX. This beautiful church is located right downtown at 2215 Ross Ave. Jim and I parked and walked around the building until we found the door to go in. This church is beautiful. You should see the organ pipes! People were inside kneeling and praying. Jim and I quietly walked around looking at all the stained glass windows, the statues, and then we knelt down to pray. We found where they were having First Friday Eucharistic Adoration, and we went in there to pray also. We read the historical markers and walked out into a hallway where they had all kinds of brochures. I brought several of them home with me. Just listen to the titles of the brochures.

1. Abortion
After Care—Healing/The Rachel Ministries in Dallas, TX
(214)544-CARE(2273) Helpline
(972)679-4760 Espanol
(817)923-4757 Ft. Worth area
healing@racheldallas.org
www.racheldallas.org

2. Project Joseph
An Outreach to Men Suffering from Abortion
Abortion After Care—Healing Diocese of Dallas, TX
(469)416-2101 or
healing@projectjosephdallas.org

3. Convert-to-Life/Sidewalk Counseling
Rescue those who are being dragged to death (Proverbs 24:11)
Catholic Pro-Life Committee of North Texas
Respect Life Ministry of the Diocese of Dallas Convert@prolifedallas.org
(972)267-LIFE(5433)
www.prolifedallas.org

I felt overwhelmed as I looked through these brochures! I am just so thankful that there are so many places for people to call, go online, or go visit to receive the healing and answers they need. There was also a flyer for the upcoming Rachel's Vineyard Retreats.

For services or more information with assurance of confidentiality, contact:
214-544-Care (Dallas), 972-679-4760 (en Espanol) 817-923-4757 (Fort Worth)
healing@racheldallas.org or sanacion@racheldallas.org (en Espanol)

Retreats for men only/Retiros para los hombres solamente
Project Joseph / Proyecto Jose: www.projectjosephdallas.org 469-416-2101

Tomorrow I will tell you all about the Catholic Church in Jefferson, TX, where we will attend Mass! (This post was written when we got back from our trip so we had already attended Mass.) I hope you all have a wonderful Friday evening. I'm going to close with some of the facts listed on the back of one of the brochures:

- Approximately 30 abortions are performed daily in the city of Dallas
- Over 9,750 abortions are performed yearly in Dallas County
- Sidewalk counselors assist approximately 900 women each year to choose life over abortion
- Planned Parenthood is the largest abortion provider in the world
- 33 percent of Planned Parenthood's annual budget is funded by taxpayers

- More than 50 percent of teenage girls who abort their first pregnancy will develop breast cancer
- The Susan G. Komen Foundation (Race for the Cure) donates funds to Planned Parenthood and does not acknowledge the abortion–breast cancer link

"I call heaven and earth today to witness against you: I have set before you life and death, the blessing and the curse. Choose life, then, that you and your descendants may live" (Deuteronomy 30:19).

Bye for now.
Sharla

There Is No Place Like Home!

Friday, June 19, 2015

Good morning out there! Today is Friday, and I hope you all have a really great day, a day full of blessings! In my previous post, I wrote about the vacation that Jim and I took. I told you about the beautiful cathedral shrine of Our Lady of Guadalupe in Dallas, TX. Today I'm going to tell you about our trip to Jefferson, TX, the Catholic Church, and the priceless (to me) pictures we bought at an antique store.

Jefferson is a beautiful little town, full of history, and northeast of Dallas. They were having a corvette show on Main Street that Saturday morning. Jim and I walked up and down the street looking at all the old and new, shiny, and colorful corvettes. The proud owners were sitting in chairs behind their cars or polishing them with a rag, telling people all about the statistics and stuff. In the distance over the top of a building, I spotted a bell tower and told Jim that I bet that was where the Catholic Church was. So we started walking towards the church, and sure enough, the beautiful old white church with the bell tower was Immaculate Conception Catholic Church. We went up the steps and through the front door. The priest was inside making sure everything was just right. He was fixing to go out of town, and so there would be a visiting priest celebrating Mass that Saturday evening and the next morning. He told us to take our time and that he was going to lock the front door, so if we would please go out the side door when we were through and just make sure it locked behind us. Jim and I walked up and down the inside of the church, admiring the amazing stained glass windows. The windows told the story of the life of Jesus. One window pane was of the Annunciation, the next was the Visitation, the birth of Christ—all scenes from the Joyful Mysteries. Then there was the pane showing the wedding at Cana, one of the Luminous Mysteries. The Crucifixion and the Pieta were two more of the beautiful but heartbreaking stained glass panes. The entire church was so breathtaking. Jim and I knelt down and prayed, and even though we were the only ones there, we whispered when we wanted to point something out. Finally, we walked out the side door and made sure it was locked. We walked back around to the front of the church and checked the Mass schedule and decided that we would come back for the 5:30 p.m. evening Mass that night. I took a picture of two signs they had at the side of the church.

One said,

> PREGNANT AND NEED HELP?
> (Mujer Embarazada y Necesita Ayuda?)
> The Catholic Church sees the birth of each baby as God's unfailing love. We offer immediate & practical help to any woman faced with crisis pregnancy
> 888-300-5112

The picture next to the words is the beautiful Madonna of the Streets.

The next sign read,

> Society of St. Vincent de Paul
> Immaculate Heart of Mary Conference
> The Society of St. Vincent de Paul offers tangible assistance to those in need on a person to person basis.

We walked back to our truck, both of us realizing what really matters, what is really important, and what and who God cares about. Taking care of one another, carrying each other's burdens, lending a helping hand is what matters. We passed an old antique store and walked in. In one room, high upon a shelf, dusty and dirty, were two old pictures.

One was the beautiful Madonna of the Streets, and the other was a picture of Jesus I had never seen before, his face in the middle and small scenes of his life all around the edge. I told Jimmy, "We have to rescue them and take them home." Jim smiled and reached up and carefully handed them to me. The owner commented on how beautiful they were and that she had never even noticed them. She carefully wrapped them up for us, and $35 later, they were safely tucked in the backseat of our truck! That evening, Jim and I did go to Mass at The Immaculate Conception Catholic Church. We walked through the doors, dipped our fingers in the holy water, made the sign of the cross, genuflected, and knelt down to pray. There truly is no place like home. May your day be full of blessings!

Bye for now.
Sharla

Mother Mary (Mama Mary) and My Little Joan

Friday, June 26, 2015

Good morning, y'all! I was listening to our Catholic radio station yesterday, 91.5 FM KPDE, on my way home from the noon Mass. The program was "Called to Communion" with Dr. David Anders. A Protestant called in and asked why we worship Mother Mary. I just want to share my thoughts on this much-asked question. I was raised Methodist, and one day, I met the most wonderful Catholic man who was very devout in his faith. I told him that I would go to Mass with him and see what I thought. I really wanted us to go to church together as a family. I fell in love with the Catholic faith (I had already fallen in love with and married the wonderful man!), and in 1986, I began taking RCIA classes. I was confirmed as a Catholic during the Easter Vigil in 1987. Now back to the reason I am writing this story, back to Mama Mary. I attached a picture to go with my story when I posted it on my Facebook page and on my blog. I picked this picture because this is how I see Mother Mary, as a loving, respected, precious mother. She is holding Jesus on her lap, and four children are at her feet. One is standing holding a bouquet of flowers. One is sitting back on her feet, her hands placed in a prayerful position, looking up at Baby Jesus and Mother Mary. The other two are kneeling with their heads bowed reverently. It is such a beautiful picture, one of my favorites. It was painted by Giuseppe

Magni (1869–1956). We do not worship Mother Mary, but we do see her for the very important person that she was and still is. God chose her to give birth to His Son. She is a wonderful example for us to follow. We ask Mother Mary to pray and intercede for us. Just like you might ask someone who has a lot of faith to pray for you, we ask Mother Mary to pray for us. She wants to bring us closer to her Son. When I look at this picture, I think about when my granddaughter Joan was in the hospital and so very sick. I remember walking over to Sacred Heart Cathedral. I walked into the sanctuary and went to the side where they have the Shrine of Our Lady of Guadalupe (picture of Our Lady of Guadalupe, the candles, and the kneeler). I lit a candle and knelt down. I was so overcome with worry that I sat back on my heels and lay my head down on my arms on the armrest of the kneeler and began to cry. I asked Mama Mary to please pray for my little Joan. I just remember crying and praying and asking her to please pray for healing, to please pray that the doctors would find out what was wrong, to please pray for me to have strength to help my daughter, her husband, and their daughters, my granddaughters. I felt like I was sitting at Mother Mary's feet, my head in her lap. My mom died when I was twelve years old, and at that moment, I really needed my mom. Mother Mary is a mom to me. She is a beautiful example of love, compassion, selflessness, and faith.

When I finished asking for her prayers, I walked up to the kneeler in front of the Tabernacle and knelt down and prayed to Jesus. I knelt quietly for a while, just taking in His presence, His peace, His comfort, and then I knew I could go back to the hospital and be strong for my family once more. I have a picture of Joan sitting on the kneeler beneath the picture of Our Lady of Guadalupe. She calls her Mama Mary, and even though at that time, she wasn't yet two years old, it was like she knew that she needed to sit at Mama Mary's feet and ask for her prayers. Our God is an awesome God, and He is who we worship, and He is who answers our prayers, and

Mother Mary intercedes for us and leads us closer to Jesus. Joan is three years and two months old now. She is doing very well, thanks be to God. She loves to go to Mass. She loves Mama Mary, but she has also started kneeling somewhere else now. When her mom goes up to receive Communion and Joan receives a blessing, she tugs free of her mom's hand when they get close to the Tabernacle. Little Joan goes to the kneeler and kneels down, and she places her little hands together in prayer, so very serious. When I see her do that, my heart stops beating for just a second because I know that Mama Mary is leading Joan to her Son.

At one point, children were brought to him so that he could place his hands on them in prayer. The disciples began to scold them, but Jesus said, "Let the children come to me. Do not hinder them. The kingdom of God belongs to such as these." And he laid his hands on their heads before he left that place. (Matthew 19:13–15)

Family, Praise, Blessings and Prayers

Wednesday, July 8, 2015

Hello out there! Thank you, God, for the rain! Just a quick post to say hello! Our two granddaughters who live out of town were with us all last week, Sunday, June 18, 2015, to Sunday, July 5, 2015. We had so much fun and enjoyed having them spend time with us. Lots of activities, busy days, family time with all the cousins and aunts and uncles, and, of course, us! Our youngest grandson turned five, so we went to his very fun birthday party! Swimming, going to the library, and Fourth of July barbecue and fireworks at Nana and Pa's place. We listened to Junie B. Jones CDs as we ran errands and just had a great week! Mealtimes, bath times, bedtime prayers, washing clothes, and brushing hair! I keep two types of Band-Aids on hand, Doc McStuffins and Minions. We went through a lot of those too! I forgot to mention the tee-ball game and jumping on the trampoline, feeding chickens, and gathering eggs! I hope you all had a wonderful week! I have to go wash the dishes now! I want to close with a prayer that was in one of my previous posts. Blessings to you all!

I just have to add; I am so blessed to have ten grandchildren!

Grandchild number 4, one of my eight granddaughters, will turn eight at the end of this month! Another birthday party, swimming, and fun! They grow up so fast! Hug them tight! Pray with them, and kiss them good night!

**July 4, 2015 – Summer Memories
with Our Grandchildren!**

I Will Speak Up for the Weakest among Us, I Will Be Their Voice!

Thursday, July 9, 2015

Hello out there! I wrote a letter and e-mailed it to the *Standard Times Newspaper* editorial department yesterday morning. My letter was in response to the guest editorial that was published the day before. The editorial had previously appeared in *The Los Angeles Times*. The title of the article was "In Texas Abortion Case, High Court Ruled Correctly." I read the article late Tuesday afternoon, and I knew that I had to write a response. That evening, I sat down with my dictionary, the article, and my literature on pro-life issues and documents about what happens during an abortion. I jotted down notes, read and reread information, cried, and then wrote some more. Jim finally said, "Sharla, you need to get some sleep. You can finish in the morning." I knew he was right. I was beyond tired and was really distressed after reading all the horrible things I knew I had to read so that I could be brutally honest in my reply. I got ready for bed and said my prayers, praying that I could write something that people would understand. I tossed and turned. I finally told Jim that I had to get up. I had to finish what I had started. He understood and gave me a hug. I gathered up all my material, my notes, and reading glasses and closed our bedroom door and came into my office. I sat down and just started typing from my heart. I looked at my notes, glanced at the article, and typed some more. I knew that my letter was way too long for the section in the newspaper designated for Letters to the Editor, but there was nothing I could cut, nothing I would cut from my rebuttal to that heartless article that I was replying to. I glanced at the clock, and it was almost 2:00 a.m. I knew that I had to get some sleep, so I saved my draft and went to bed. I prayed the Divine Mercy Chaplet and finally fell asleep. Jim didn't wake me when he got up, and when he came to kiss me good-bye before he went to work, I jumped up and said, "Wait, you have to read my article first!" I stumbled around for a minute, and he said, "Why don't I go and fix you a cup of coffee while you get everything together." He knows me so well. Bless his sweet, patient heart! I sat down and clicked on my draft on the computer, and Jim sat down next to me. I read my letter to him so he would get all the emphasis on the really important parts. He told me it was great, that I needed to send it to more than just our newspaper. He hoped they would print it and said that he really had to get to work because he was running late! I typed a note to the person I was sending the article to and asked if there was a place they could print it since it was long. I heard back from him about noon, and he said that he would shoot for next Thursday's View Points section.

Here is a brief description of the article I read: There was not one word in their letter about the babies who are killed during abortions. It was full of statistics and laws. They compared the safety of having an abortion to other outpatient procedures, such as laser eye surgery, dental extractions, colonoscopies, and vasectomies. They didn't talk about any possible side effects of having an abortion. The letter basically stated that this is the law of the land, so accept it and shut up.

Now back to my response.

This is one of the points I made. I just can't believe the audacity of the comparison of having an abortion to laser eye surgery or having a tooth extracted. What part of "a baby is dead" do you not get? Doctors are supposed to heal, not kill.

I have to say, my blood was pumping, my heart was beating like a jackhammer, and I was taking notes like I knew shorthand. But you see, that's just it. I have a heart, and I felt like it was breaking. My response tells the ugly truth about abortion. My response talks about the babies and the grief that so many feel after having an abortion. My response talks about all the possible side effects of having an abortion and what really happens during an abortion. My response is about humanity and love, and it comes from my heart.

I will speak up for the weakest among us. I will be their voice.

As a Couple, Being Pro-Life Is Our Way of Life

Monday, July 20, 2015

Hello out there! It is a balmy one-hundred-something degrees this afternoon, and the week ahead looks hot, hot, and hot! Now that I've given you the weather forecast for San Angelo, I will begin my story.

I just have to share this awesome, peaceful feeling I have right now. If you have been following my blog for a while, you know that I write about my family, my faith, and my pro-life advocacy. Speaking up for the unborn and spreading the pro-life message is definitely my mission. Making sure I post updated websites about adoption, pregnancy help centers, and healing after an abortion is very important to me. I have also written about a baby's gestation from conception to birth, a true miracle that I love to share. Something I don't like to think about, much less write about, but have to, is how horrible an abortion truly is, what takes place, and possible complications during and/or after an abortion.

This fall will be my third time to lead a 40 Days for Life Campaign here in San Angelo. Since the Planned Parenthood here shut down, we pray in the outside courtyard of our parish, Sacred Heart Cathedral. Several of my previous blog posts are about things that happen during the campaigns.

Now back to my awesome, peaceful feeling. Many times, I have prayed and asked God if I was doing enough. "Am I headed in the right direction? Are You really sure You want me to lead a campaign?"

I knew in my heart that God wanted me to really get involved and speak up for the unborn, but then I would start doubting that I was doing a good job. I would start second-guessing myself, but I kept on fighting for the babies; I didn't give up. I posted a picture on Facebook of Blessed Mother Teresa, and the quote says, "God has not called me to be Successful. He called me to be Faithful." I have shared that picture many times, and I have read the words she spoke many more times. I finally get it. I finally get it!

This past Sunday morning, Jim and I got up and got ready. We pulled out two of the vinyl pro-life banners, made sure we had the zip ties and scissors, and we loaded everything up in the truck. We headed to the courtyard, our mission planned out. We prayed for our family on the way. We had to circle the block to find a parking place because it was almost time for the 10:00 a.m. Mass. We parked, gathered our supplies, and crossed the street. We passed people who were hurrying to get to Mass as we were going to the courtyard. We went to the gate and took down the pro-life banner that we had hung up three weeks before. We carefully folded it back up and hung up the new one. This banner has a black background, and on one side, there is a picture of a baby in the womb being cradled by a pair of hands, and the quote on the other side says, "It is a poverty to decide that a child must die so that you may live as you wish."

This quote is also by Blessed Mother Teresa, my hero.

Jim and I stood back and looked at the banner after we hung it up. The banners are really large, eight feet long three and a half feet high. I backed up and took a picture. I sat down on some steps behind me so that I could get a good shot. After I took the picture, I said a little prayer. I felt choked up, and tears came to my eyes. Jim put up the banner we had taken down, and we walked around to the front side of the courtyard to hang up the next banner. An older woman in a motorized wheelchair came down the sidewalk right next to us. She told us how she loves to stop and look at the banners every day when she passes by. Jim and I thanked her and told her that we were so glad that she liked them. I reached out and touched her arm before she drove away. We went through the same routine—took down one banner and hung another one up. This banner has a white background, and one side says, "I'm a Child, Not a Choice!" The other side has the face of a beautiful baby. The atmosphere while Jim and I were quietly working was so peaceful. Our work was done with a quiet reverence, knowing we were doing what God has called us to do.

That evening, we arrived early for the 6:00 p.m. Mass. We looked at the banners and watered the flowers we had planted. It was early when we walked into the cathedral. We were the only ones in the sanctuary as we knelt down to pray. Mass was wonderful; it always is.

This morning, when Jim and I were praying at the Adoration Chapel, I finally realized what God was telling me.

I wish I could describe the peace I feel in my heart, the joy and love I feel when we are speaking up for the unborn, when Jim and I are working together to get the pro-life message out there. Knowing with absolute certainty that this is what *we*, as a couple, have been called to do is both humbling and awesome at the same time. I am sharing this with you to ask for your prayers. Please pray for Jim and me as we continue speaking out for the unborn because I finally realized that our mission is going to be a very busy day-to-day pro-life way of life.

I'm going to close with a prayer I read this morning in my *Living Faith* daily Catholic devotions book. It is one of the morning prayers in the back. "Lead me, Lord, to new experiences of faith today. When I find myself in doubt, nudge me gently forward and walk beside me. You have blessed me with courage and compassion that I may follow your holy way. Thank you for trusting me to love as you love. Amen."

Bye for now.
Sharla

Listen to Your Heart
Don't Listen to the World!

Saturday, August 1, 2015

Hello out there! The last couple of weeks have been full of reports about the scandal at Planned Parenthood. I have watched the tapes, read the reports, watched the news, and now I'm ready to share how I see this situation. First of all, I'm appalled, disgusted, horrified, upset, dismayed, and just downright sad. I pray that these heartbreaking videos will open the eyes of the blind so that they can truly see the evil that lies within the walls of Planned Parenthood.

I have commented on many of the pro-life posts that have come out on Facebook about the scandal. I am happy to share that there are many people trying to get the pro-life message out. I have shared comments back and forth with both men and women who have suffered greatly because of a past abortion. My heart goes out to all of them. I shared websites for healing after an abortion. I also heard from other people who were adopted and one lady who shared her story of being a birth mother. She knew that she would not be able to care for her baby and chose adoption. She and I replied back and forth for quite a while. I told her that since I couldn't thank my own birth mother, I wanted her to know that she did good! I told her that I knew she loved her baby and did what she thought was best for her child. Our back-and-forth dialogue was pretty emotional for me.

Dear, God, please open our eyes and touch our hearts. Please have mercy on us all. Amen.

So many people share their grief over a past abortion that I posted websites for Rachel's Vineyard Retreats. Please share these websites. You never know who might need them.

www.rachelsvineyard.org

www.hopeafterabortion.com

www.abortionrecovery.org

For men: healing@projectjosephdallas.org or call (469) 416-2101

May your weekend be full of blessings.

Bye for now.

Sharla

Happy Birthday, Homemade Banana Pudding, and a Love Story

Friday, August 7, 2015

Good morning out there! Yesterday was my husband's birthday, and I am just so thankful for him. He is such a blessing to me, our children, and our grandchildren! Instead of a birthday cake, I made banana pudding using the original, old-fashioned recipe. I had to double the recipe because we have such a big family, and I used one entire box of Nilla Wafer and three quarters of another box because Jim likes the cookies! I carefully arranged each layer in a nine-by-thirteen casserole dish. The original recipe has meringue on top, so you have to cook it for about twenty minutes. When I pulled it out of the oven, it was browned just right! While the pudding was cooling, I seasoned a brisket and put it in the oven to cook. I already had a big pot of red beans (pinto beans) cooking! I washed up some of the dishes, and then I placed vanilla wafers all around the edge of the pudding and put a few on top in the middle. I placed the banana pudding on the table and covered it with a couple of napkins. I moved the beans to the backburner and started another pot of water boiling on the front burner to cook the pasta for a pasta salad. I wanted to hurry and get that done so that I could get it in the fridge to cool before dinner.

So the dessert is on the table, the brisket is cooking, the beans are simmering, and the pasta salad is in the fridge. I decide to go ahead and cook some pork ribs too! I take them out of the fridge, season them, wrap them in foil, and put them in the oven on top of the brisket.

Dishes are washed, dinner is cooking, and dessert is made. I stock the fridge with drinks and take out the trash. I really need to take a break for a few minutes, but I think of something else I need to do. Before I know it, my husband is home from work, and the kids and grandkids arrive shortly thereafter.

Hugs and kisses and "Happy Birthday, Pa" before the kids head out the backdoor to jump on the trampoline and/or jump in the metal stock tank we have for them to splash around in. While they are busy playing, the dads set up a table and chairs in the backyard while the moms fix the kid's plates. Prayers are said, and everyone is fed!

Our daughter made brownies with lots of pecans because that is how Jim likes them. Our son brought watermelons that we will eat this weekend when our oldest son and his family come to celebrate again.

With full tummies and tired kids, hugs and kisses once more, everyone loaded up to head back to their homes. Jim and I walked back into the house, our home, smiled, and took a deep breath. We finished straightening up, feeling very blessed. I bought a rustic-looking picture/sign that I hung out on the back porch this week. It says, "Every love story is beautiful, but ours is my favorite." Jim says it is the perfect sign for us!

Blessings to you and yours!

Bye for now.

Sharla

This Little Light of Mine
I'm Going to Try
and Let It Shine!

Monday, August 24, 2015

Good morning out there! Prayers are being said for all the children, teens, teachers, counselors, bus drivers, and everyone else who works in our schools! Today was the first day of school for six of my grandchildren. My youngest grandson is in kindergarten, one of my granddaughters is in first grade, and another granddaughter is in third grade. My three oldest grandchildren are all in the fourth grade (one grandson and two granddaughters). I have two more granddaughters who will be going to Mother's Day Out programs, and the youngest two granddaughters (five and a half months and almost five months) are still at home with their moms! Yes, the girls outnumber the boys four to one!

Last night before Mass, I bought candles. I carried the candles over to the Shrine of Our Lady of Guadalupe. I said the name of each one of my grandchildren as I lit a candle for them. I knelt down to pray and looked at all the candles burning brightly. I looked up at the beautiful picture of Our Lady of Guadalupe and smiled. As I prayed for each one of my grandchildren, I thought about all the people who had lit a candle, what an awesome visual sign of faith. Prayers lifted up to God for all our intentions, always praying for those we love.

This morning, Jim and I were at the Adoration Chapel. I love the quiet, peaceful hour that we spend there early each Monday morning. I prayed the Joyful Mysteries of the Rosary and read my daily devotionals. Jim and I sit side by side. Sometimes, he is kneeling, and other times, I am. We quietly pray our own prayers. The hour that we spend with Jesus in the quiet little chapel is truly priceless.

I read something in one of my devotionals about being a light in the darkness. I hope that I am a light to those around me. May God bless you all.

Blessings and peace.

Sharla

Come! Live in the Light! Shine with the Joy and the Love of the Lord!

Thursday, September 3, 2015

Good morning out there! I hope you all are doing well! Just a quick post before I start my day. It is that time of year again. I am busy planning for the upcoming fall 40 Days for Life Campaign here in San Angelo, TX. This will be the third one that we have held in the courtyard at my parish, Sacred Heart Cathedral. So far, it is going really well. People have been calling me to sign up and ask what they can do to help! I am so thankful for all these dedicated pro-life warriors! The preparations for the kick-off rally that will be held on Tuesday, September 22, 2015, are rolling right along. I am really excited about it!

The kick-off rally will be from 6:00 p.m. to 7:30 p.m.

We will serve hot dogs, chips, drinks, and desserts!

There will be music! A DJ (a young man from our parish) will start playing music at about 5:30 p.m. and will continue right on to the end!

Our choir director and members of the music ministry will bless us with their voices and will lead us in praise and worship music!

Sidewalk chalk, balloons, fellowship, and prayers. Families and friends everywhere!

I know that it will be a wonderful evening, a great way to kick off the next 40 days.

The 40 Days for Life Campaign begins on Wednesday, September 23, 2015, and goes through Sunday, November 1, 2015.

There will be people praying in the courtyard from 7:00 a.m. to 7:00 p.m. every day. Most people sign up for a one-hour timeslot each week; some people just drop in and pray for fifteen to twenty minutes or so when they are in the area. We also have rosary groups that come and pray in the courtyard during this time. Sometimes you will walk into the courtyard, and there will be a large group of people all praying together. Other times, you will see people all spread out, praying by themselves, reading the Bible or their daily devotions. The fellowship is awesome, and the peace and serenity that resonates in the courtyard during the 40 days is such a gift, a true blessing.

I am really looking forward to this fall 40 Days for Life Campaign! There are 307 locations this time! Isn't that great? Go to the 40 Days for Life website and find a location near you! I know that you will be blessed by the experience! www.40daysforlife.com

If you want to keep up with what is happening at the 40 Days for Life in the courtyard, visit our Facebook page, 40 Days for Life - San Angelo, TX. I post lots of pictures and share news from that day!

I hope you all have a wonderful day. I am going to close with a verse from a song we sang at Mass this past weekend.

The song title is "We Are Called."

> Come! Live in the light! Shine with the joy and the love of the Lord!

> We are called to be light for the kingdom, to live in the freedom of the city of God! [Refrain] We are called to act with justice. We are called

to love tenderly. We are called to serve one another, to walk humbly with God.

I love that song!
Bye for now.
Sharla

Love, Joy, Family, and Light: Celebrating Two Baptisms

Monday, September 21, 2015

Hello out there! What a beautiful Sunday afternoon! In the past three weeks, our youngest granddaughters, number 9 and 10, have been baptized! All ten of our grandchildren have now been baptized in the Catholic Church. As the grandmother of these ten blessings from God, I couldn't be happier, and their grandfather feels the same way! The kids call us Nana and Pa, and they are all unique and precious to us. As I've said before, we have eight granddaughters and two grandsons. So the numbers I give are when they were born.

We baptized granddaughter number 10 three weeks ago after the Saturday evening Mass at Sacred Heart in the little chapel. She looked so beautiful in her white baptism gown. What made it even more special, she wore the same gown her oldest sister (number 3) wore when she was baptized, also at Sacred Heart but in the big sanctuary. I wish you could have heard the other grandkids voices as we prayed the Our Father during the baptism. From the smallest to the tallest, their little voices praying in one accord will stay in my heart forever.

We all went out to eat afterwards: our daughter, her husband, and their three little girls, including number 10, the shining star of the evening, and our son, his wife, their three little girls, and two sons our only grandsons! We ate at a Mexican restaurant with several tables pushed together. I smile when I think of all the laughing and joy that evening held. One of my favorite moments was when we all prayed together before we ate our meal, giving thanks to God for everything.

We baptized granddaughter number 9 after the 11:00 a.m. Mass today! She was baptized at St. Boniface Catholic Church in Olfen. She was also beautiful in her white baptism gown. What made it even more special, she wore the same gown her oldest sister (number 4) wore when she was baptized. My heart was touched again as we prayed in one accord, the smallest to the tallest, their sweet voices heard. Both baptisms were beautiful, and the babies did so well. It was like they knew that this was something special, something powerful, something that must be done. I want to share something else that touched my heart today. Grandson number 1 and granddaughter number 3 (cousins) were sitting side by side in the pew in front of my husband and me at Mass today. They are nine years old now, and when I saw them, I thought of a time not so long ago when his father and her mother sat side by side at Mass learning to follow God to grow up in His ways.

Yes, today was a blessing. My husband and I, two of our adult children, and their families all at Mass together, celebrating another baptism, continuing to try and follow God's ways.

We went out to eat at a different Mexican restaurant today, our large, happy family, including number 9, the shining star of the day. Crowded tables blessed with food and also laughter, love, and thankfulness!

Blessings to you and yours!

Bye for now.
Sharla

Prayers and Blessings!
Blessings and Prayers!

Friday, September 25, 2015

Good evening out there! The kick-off rally was great and the 40 Days for Life Campaign has begun! This has been a wonderful week! My heart has been so blessed by all the helping hands that pitched in to make the kick-off such a success. My dear pro-life friends and family helped set up tables and chairs. They set up the canopies decorated with balloons, fixed and served the hotdogs, and kept the ice chests stocked with waters. Cookies and brownies were brought by the families, and some people dropped off cookies even though they weren't able to stay.

One of my best friends met me at HEB to buy the groceries for the rally. We had so much fun, and you would not believe the coupons and sales that were exactly for what we needed! Our God is an awesome God, and we saved so much money at the store. You won't believe this, but HEB had coupons for the cutest little children's books, many of them Bible stories, and we got twenty-four of them for free! We were so excited, and we were able to give each family with children a beautiful book at the rally! The music ministry from our parish outdid themselves with praise and worship songs. They passed out song sheets, and we sang along. We also got up and did the hand motions and danced to many. The children danced and colored the courtyard pavement with creative and thought-provoking sidewalk chalk pictures and messages. We had students from the Pro-Life Rams and the Newman Center from the college come and join us. They seemed to have a great time. The courtyard is in the downtown area, and a couple of the homeless men stopped by to see what was going on. We invited them to come and eat, and they did! One of them even stayed and helped us put up the chairs and tables, an absolutely great way to start the 40 days!

I drove up to the courtyard on Wednesday morning at about 6:50 a.m. There were already three people praying! Every day has been a blessing! Yesterday, the moms' group held their weekly meeting in the courtyard. There were four beautiful young women, one expecting her second son soon. There were two baby girls and two toddler boys! Listening to their laughter and squeals made me smile. I looked out from where I was sitting and noticed a man who comes to get a lunch from the Sack Lunch Ministry sitting on one of the benches. Another man, a parishioner, was praying the rosary. The moms were visiting, the toddlers were playing, and I just thought what a perfect picture!

I have to go and wash the dishes now. I'll keep you posted about the blessings in the courtyard! Have a wonderful weekend, and please take just a moment each day to say a prayer for the unborn, for babies, for families everywhere!

"Let all that you do be done in love" (1 Corinthians 16:14).

Bye for now.
Sharla

Happy Fall, Y'all!
Saved By Grace and Jesus, Protect and Save the Unborn!

Thursday, October 1, 2015

Hello, hello out there! Today has been a beautiful day! I have a small flag hanging by my front porch that says, "Happy Fall, Y'all!" I laugh every time I read it because it sounds like it was made just for me! Now back to the serious, awesome stuff going on in my life! In my post yesterday, I was going to tell you about two more things that happened last week, but I only had time to tell you one of the stories. So here is the second story.

I've told y'all about the kick-off rally and shopping for the groceries at HEB and how we saved so much money and the precious children's books we got for free with our coupons. This is what happened next.

I am driving out of the HEB parking lot at about 12:30 p.m., and I remember that I wanted to get a personalized pro-life T-shirt. Keep in mind, I need to be at the courtyard by 3:00 p.m. to start setting up for the rally. I drive down the street to an athletic store, park, and run inside. I explain to the young lady that I know I waited until the last minute, but is there any way I can buy a T-shirt and have the word *adopted* printed across the front and pick it up by 2:30 p.m.? She goes into the back and checks and then lets me know that they will be able to do it. She brings out different colors of T-shirts for me to pick from. I pick hot pink and ask if I can have something printed on the back also. She says, "Yes," and so I am standing there talking to myself trying to think of what I want on the back. I don't even realize that the young lady is paying any attention to me until she says, "How about, 'saved by grace'?" My eyes fill up with tears, and I reach across the counter and pat her arm and tell her that she is an angel. She tells me not to cry because she will start crying too! Isn't that the most amazing thing? I tell her why I'm buying the shirt and invite her to come and join us in the courtyard. I pay for my shirt and tell her that I will be back at 2:30 p.m. I call my friend, Candi, on the way home and tell her what just happened. She had been shopping with me at HEB. Anyway, I go home and get ready. I pick up my shirt on the way to the courtyard, and then I pick up one of the teenagers who is going to help set up. My husband meets us up at the courtyard, and other people arrive to help also. My friend, Candi, arrives in a baby blue T-shirt and turns around so I can read the print on the back. "Jesus, Protect and Save the Unborn!" is what it said. She told me that after I called her, she went to the same store and bought her own personalized T-shirt because she wanted to surprise me! I just hugged her. She is such a blessing to me!

I've already told y'all how wonderful the rally was, how thankful I am for all my wonderful friends and my sweet, supportive family. I love sharing this story with all of you.

I pray that you are all blessed with love and laughter, with hugs and tears. I pray that you are blessed with family and friends, and, most importantly, the knowledge that God loves *you* so very much.

Life is a gift from God, and how we live our life is our gift back to God. Blessings, blessings to you and yours!

Bye for now.

Sharla

Pray, Speak Up, Don't Give Up!

Friday, October 9, 2015

Good morning out there! It rained yesterday afternoon and last night. I'm always thankful for the rain! It is nice and cool outside this morning, overcast and looks like we may receive some more showers. That is enough about the weather forecast. I don't have much time, so I have to move on to the next item!

It has been a wonderful week in the courtyard: beautiful weather, awesome people, super great kids, and sidewalk chalk drawings and messages that will grab your heart and bring tears to your eyes! Praying for an end to abortion, praying for the babies, born and unborn. We have been praying for the mothers, praying for the fathers, and just praying for families everywhere. I have to share this one story with you. There is a mom who brings her children with her to pray. Her daughter is nine, and her son is preschool age. They pray the Pro-Life Rosary, and the children draw with the sidewalk chalk. I wasn't in the courtyard during the time they stopped by to pray, but I knew that they had been there without even looking at the sign-in sheet. I saw a chalk-drawn picture of a lady with a tear on her cheek, and the message said, "Abortion hurts the mothers too." The other picture was of Spiderman, and the message said, "Spiderman will adopt the babies." I smiled, kind of a sad smile, because it hurt my heart that these beautiful children truly see the ugly truth about abortion. Their sweet little hearts know the truth.

When I see the young mothers out there praying with their little ones, sometimes pushing them in a stroller around and around the courtyard as they pray, I smile, and I thank God. When I see the teenagers out there praying, I smile, and I thank God. When I see people my age and older in the courtyard praying, I smile, and I thank God. When I hear the laughter of little ones playing in the courtyard, I smile, and I thank God. Last night, I went to the Pregnancy Help Center dinner/banquet. I'm a table host, and the early fundraising event is always enjoyable. The Pregnancy Help Center does exactly what their name says; it helps young ladies and women (and their precious babies too).

This is a really important thing to remember: pregnancy help centers do not take any money from you. They truly want to help you and your baby. Planned Parenthood is a business, and they only care about the money you will pay them. The abortion industry is a money-making business. Don't forget that. I hear the pro-abortion people tell women that they can be anything they want to be, but then they tell them that they aren't capable of taking care of their own child? What kind of sick advice is that?

I am here to tell you that your child is a gift, a miracle, a human being, and *you are strong enough, you are capable enough, and there are people who will help you take care of your baby! Being a mom is a gift, and if you aren't ready, adoption is a loving life option. Please, choose life!*

Well, I guess y'all know how I feel. I have to get ready to head to the courtyard. I wish that every day I could write about something silly and lighthearted. I wish that I could just bring a smile to your face. But I have to write what is in my heart. I have to be honest. This blog is my way of trying to do something, trying to reach someone, and praying that God will guide my hands and that I will type His words.

Bye for now.

Sharla

Praying for the Conversion of Hearts

Wednesday, October 14, 2015

Good morning out there! It is beautiful outside! The sun is shining, and there is a cool breeze in the air. I love the weather in the fall! I only have time for a quick post, but I just have to share this with y'all before I head out the door to the courtyard! I posted a picture to go with this story. (The story is from Monday and Tuesday.)

A couple of years ago, Jim and I visited some of the painted churches east of San Antonio.

This picture was taken in Praha, (Flatonia) at St. Mary's, The Assumption of The Blessed Virgin Mary Catholic Church. The grotto outside was beautiful. I love this picture of my husband, Jim, reaching up and holding our Blessed Mother's hands. He really sees things in a better light than I do most of the time. Here is a current example: Monday night, Jim tells me that he has felt a tug at his heart to pray for Cecile Richards (CEO of Planned Parenthood), to pray that her heart be softened.

He tells me to ask the people praying in the courtyard to pray for her. I think that this is a great idea, so I spread the word to please pray for a conversion of heart for her. Everyone is on board. One of my sweet friends said that, of course, we should pray for her. Not one person was negative. Now here is the rest of the story and probably why I need to go to confession Wednesday afternoon! A couple of hours ago (Tuesday evening), Jim and I were visiting, and I told him that I asked everyone to pray for Cecile Richards, and then I told him my prayer (this is where going to confession comes in). I told him that I prayed that she would have a dream where she stands in heaven and all the babies who have been killed from abortion flash before her and that she sees the flames of hell below her and that God tells her that she must change to enter the kingdom of heaven and that the dream would truly scare the hell right out of her! Jim looked kind of shocked and said, "I was just talking about praying for a conversion of heart, but I guess if that is what it takes!" Anyway, my prayer was probably not appropriate, but I just want her to realize how horrible abortion is, and so you know, I will be in confession on Wednesday, telling our priest how praying for that was not nice and that we should just pray that her eyes be opened and her heart be touched!

Dear God, thank you for my husband, who is such a good and devout man and truly cares for everyone and is always praying for everyone. Please help me to have a more open heart. Amen.

Please do pray for everyone to realize the true horror and death that abortion brings. Please pray for all who work in the abortion business to have a change of heart. A baby's heart starts beating just eighteen days after conception. Isn't that amazing?

I hope you all have a wonderful day!

Blessings,

Sharla

Yes, They'll Know We Are Christians by Our Love!

Monday, November 2, 2015

Hello out there! It is 1:43 a.m., and I am wide awake! The closing celebration for the fall 40 Days for Life Campaign was yesterday, and I was so tired when we came home from Mass last night. I was in bed and sound asleep by 9:30 p.m. About 12:45 a.m., I woke up and knew that I wouldn't be going back to sleep anytime soon. I prayed and then thought about all the loose ends I need to tie up today. Since I wasn't at all sleepy, I decided to sit down and write a post!

How are y'all doing out there? I pray that you are all well and that your week will be blessed! I can't believe that the fall 40 Days Campaign has ended. We started off with a great kick-off rally followed by 40 days of prayerful vigil, fellowship, laughter, and tears. We closed out the fall campaign yesterday afternoon right before the evening Mass. The closing celebration was very nice, kind of low key, but a wonderful blessing and great way to end a very busy forty-ish days! There ended up being about twenty-eight people at the closing celebration, and we served cookies, coffee, and bottled water. Frank, our wonderful music ministry leader, led us in three beautiful and perfect songs.

"Blest Are They" was the first song he sang, and we joined in for the refrain. "Rejoice and be glad! Blessed are you, holy are you! Rejoice and be glad! Yours is the kingdom of God!"

"We Are Called" was the second song, and this is the refrain: "We are called to act with justice. We are called to love tenderly. We are called to serve one another, to walk humbly with God."

"They'll Know We Are Christians" was the third song and the refrain is, "And they'll know we are Christians by our love, by our love. Yes, they'll know we are Christians by our love."

Frank picked out the most perfect songs for our closing celebration. Singing together outside in the courtyard and sharing some of our experiences during the 40 days was a beautiful and peaceful way to close out the fall campaign.

My friend, Candi, who has also been my right hand during this campaign, helped me write out "save the date" cards for the 2016 spring campaign, and we handed them out along with stapled copies of the prayers we pray during the vigil hours. The leftover cookies and bottled waters are being donated to the Sack Lunch Ministry, which our parish provides to those in need, Monday through Friday from 11:00 a.m. to 1:00 p.m.

I think I am finally getting sleepy, so I am going to go ahead and close for now. I'll write another post about all the wonderful people and families who came out to pray in a couple more days. God bless you all! Pray for families everywhere, please especially pray for those in a crisis pregnancy, and please pray for their unborn babies.

Bye for now.
Sharla

Promoting Adoption: Sharing My Story

Wednesday, November 4, 2015

Dad and the Banker

Good morning out there! November is National Adoption Month. I wrote a story about my adoption awhile back. I want to share it with you today. Promoting adoption as a life option is very important to me. I hope you enjoy this heart-warming story from a time not so long ago! I've always loved the stories about my adoption. When I was a little girl, my dad would tell me how they got the call sooner than they expected and how they had to stop and buy diapers, bottles, and clothes on the way to get me from the hospital. My mom, dad, big brother, and my grandmother all drove from Stephenville, TX, where my grandparents lived, to Ft. Worth, TX, to pick me up! My dad would say that they picked me out special from all the babies in the hospital; of course, as I grew older, I realized that part of the story was a very sweet addition. When I started asking more detailed questions, my mom said that my birth mother wasn't able to take care of me, and so she gave me to a family who could. My mom also told me that being adopted was special and that I should always be thankful, and I am.

After I grew up and had a family of my own, my dad told me how they paid for my adoption. I was born in the evening on December 30, 1963. My parents received a phone call on New Year's Eve morning that there was a baby girl ready for them. Not expecting the call quite so soon, they had to come up with the money so that they could bring me home. I need to give you a little history here so that you can get the whole picture.

My dad was a science teacher in Sudan, TX. He also drove the school bus. Sudan is a very small town close to Lubbock, TX. My dad called the banker in Sudan to request a loan and told him that he needed the money immediately. The banker asked if he had any collateral, and Dad said, "Just my name." So the banker asked my dad why he needed the money, and my dad told him that they were trying to adopt a baby girl and they were supposed to pick me up on January 2.

This is my favorite part: the banker said, "Well, go and get her. We'll figure it out when you get home." Isn't that awesome? I love it! I also have an old yellowed newspaper clipping from the Sudan newspaper telling all about the baby shower that the wonderful, gracious people gave my parents. The clipping says "Little Miss Sharla Kay, recently adopted daughter of Mr. and Mrs. Arthur Nelson, was the honoree at a shower on Saturday afternoon at the home of…"

Just writing about this makes me emotional. I've been so blessed. There is just no way to describe how thankful I am for my life. But what breaks my heart is that you don't hear about adoption anymore, unless it's for an animal. We need to get the message out there that adoption is and should be the only other option. So many couples aren't able to have children and want children.

Children are gifts from God. They are not a choice; they are a life. I love that story, and I pray that there will be more people like that banker. I pray that we will be able to get the adoption message out there. I look at my children and my grandchildren, and I am just so thankful that I was given the chance to grow up and share my story. Adoption is a loving life option, and adoption saves generations!

Please spread the beautiful truth about adoption and help me save more generations.

Blessings.
Sharla

Adoption saves generations

Without me, this is the picture you would see

I am proud to share the comment below written by my aunt, Carolyn Nelson. Aunt Carolyn was adopted when my dad was fourteen and his older brother, my uncle was sixteen years old. My aunt and I have a very special bond and I cannot imagine this world without her beautiful smile and big heart. She has been blessed with four children of her own, several grandchildren and some great grandchildren too! She was a school teacher for over thirty-five years and her students loved her.

My Aunt Carolyn wrote the following comment on my blog after reading my story about my dad and the banker.

Ouch! That post touched my heartstrings! I'm Sharla's Aunt Carolyn. I too have the clipping from the Aransas Pass, TX paper that announced to the world that Mr. and Mrs. W.M. Nelson had recently adopted a baby daughter and her name was Caroline Adele Nelson. I loved reading that clipping in my scrapbook with my name misspelled. I have had people spell it that way many times in my seventy years. The whole town and neighboring towns rallied round my parent's home bringing gifts and cards or sending them. (My mother would not allow the town to give us a shower. She had been postmaster and heard people complain about..."Oh dear, another invitation to send a gift!") The people of our fair town didn't care. They just brought them anyway. I never knew a stranger, and that was a good thing for you never knew who was going to drop in and want to hold me and feed me my bottle.

When I was almost 20 years old, my mother called me at a neighbor's house to tell me that Arthur Neil and Marty had just adopted "Little Miss Sharla Kay". I was so excited I just squealed with tears in my eyes! It wasn't long before I got to hold her and feed her, her bottles. What a joy! I was so proud of my brother, sister in love and nephew for adding to our family the same way my parents had added me to theirs.

I have always been proud of being adopted. My parents were 48 years old when they adopted me. And they lived to see all four of my children be born. Yes, 1944 was a very good year for me and my family...and so was 1963, when we were all blessed with Sharla Kay! And now I gladly join her in a pleading support of adoption. Please, save the children! Give them a chance to experience the life that has been started for them. Vote to save the children!

Hundreds of Hours Praying for the Unborn and Their Families

Sunday, November 15, 2015

Hello out there! It is cloudy and misty and a wonderful fall day! The only problem with this kind of weather is I want to hibernate and cook! Friday night, I made a *big* pot of homemade potato soup with spicy sausage, grated cheese and saltine and/or Ritz crackers on the side, and a pitcher of ice tea! Saturday morning, I started soaking pinto beans, took a brisket out of the freezer to thaw, and made a triple batch of the original Chex party mix! I cooked the beans and brisket, and that is what we had for dinner last night! This morning (Sunday), I made a big breakfast: bacon, sausage, scrambled eggs, and refried some of the beans I cooked yesterday! We had toasted tortillas also and a *big* pot of coffee! This afternoon, I made a pan of brownies with walnuts! I am supposed to be dieting before the holidays. It doesn't seem to be working out that way, but I am exercising! That has to count for something. I like to think so anyway! I only have a few more minutes before I have to get ready for Mass, so I want to share something really awesome!

I had to fill out a survey about our 40 Days for Life fall campaign. One of the questions they ask is, how many people participated (approximately)? I ask people to sign in when they come and pray; most everyone does. I went through the book and counted each individual and added some walk-ins that I knew about, and the total of people came out to 220! Isn't that awesome? Two hundred and twenty people came to the courtyard and prayed during the 40 days! I decided to count up the hours that people prayed. Most people come more than once, and the total hours came out to a little more than eight hundred! Just think about that? Eight hundred hours of prayers for the unborn and their families! There were 307 40 Days for Life campaigns, an amazing amount of prayers!

As I go up to the courtyard each day, the pro-life banners proudly hung, and the joy of seeing people praying will forever stay in my heart. Just imagine walking into a courtyard and seeing a mother praying while her children are drawing pictures and writing pro-life messages with sidewalk chalk close by. Or think about this: you walk into the courtyard, and a man is praying quietly as he sits on a bench, and a group of ladies are praying the Pro-Life Rosary together, and another lady is praying by the statue of Jesus. There were times when three generations from one family would be praying together. Other times, I witnessed a mother and her grown son praying and a grandmother and her teenage grandson praying. I would walk in and see sisters and friends praying, and the husbands and wives would sit side by side and pray. So many husbands and wives prayed together, an absolutely beautiful sight! I saw families pray together, and people would visit and laugh and share stories and sometimes cry. There were lots of hugs and a feeling of peace and serenity in the courtyard. I am thankful for every single person who stopped by to pray, who prayed from home, and who prayed for my family! I was so humbled and thankful when people told me that they were praying for Jim and me. The 40 days is over, but the pro-life way of life continues on, and we are already making plans for the spring campaign. The banners have been taken down, and the courtyard looks lonely, so stop by and say a prayer or two if you have time. Keep on praying for the unborn and their families. Keep on praying for a conversion of hearts! I am going to close with, "Jesus, protect and save the unborn," or as Jim says it, "Jesus, save and protect the unborn!"

Blessings to you and yours!

Bye for now.
Sharla

We Are Called to Serve

Monday, November 16, 2015

Good morning out there! Jim and I went to Adoration this morning at St. Margaret's Adoration Chapel. I turned the page in my *Living Faith* daily Catholic devotions to today's date, and two things just jumped right off the page and grabbed my attention. The first thing was the title, "We Are Called to Serve." Talk about grabbing my heart! Yes, we are all called to serve! One of my favorite songs from Mass is "We Are Called." I have written the lyrics to this beautiful hymn in one of my previous posts. I think it was back in September.

The second thing that caught my eye was that today, we remember Saint Margaret of Scotland, and Jim and I were at the St. Margaret of Scotland Catholic Church Adoration Chapel! I thought that was so cool! I whispered out kind of loud to Jim that information. He was kneeling and praying, so I got the look that said, "Can't this wait? I'm praying!" I just smiled and picked up my *Magnificat* because I knew that there would be a story about St. Margaret in there, and there was. She was a good wife and mother. She was married to King Malcolm III of Scotland, and they had eight children. She was very giving and kind. Everything I read about her reverted back to the title, "We Are Called to Serve"! I love that we have such wonderful examples to follow. I just wanted to share that with y'all. It was a wonderful way to start my day! Blessings to you and yours!

Bye for now.

Sharla

The song title is "We Are Called"

> Come! Live in the light! Shine with the joy and
> the love of the Lord!

> We are called to be light for the kingdom, to
> live in the freedom of the city of God!

> [Refrain] We are called to act with justice. We
> are called to love tenderly.

> We are called to serve one another, to walk
> humbly with God.

By the way, I did tell Jim all about St. Margaret on the way
home!

The First Sunday of Advent

Sunday, November 29, 2015

    Good morning out there! Today is the first Sunday of Advent! It is a cold and rainy day here in San Angelo. I hope you all had a wonderful Thanksgiving. We had a very blessed day! Family and friends joined us for a wonderful meal. The grandkids had so much fun together, and the adults enjoyed visiting. We packed up leftovers for everyone to take home. Jim and I really enjoyed our time together on Friday. It is so nice when he has some time off. No, we did not go shopping! We picked up around the house, and then we ran some errands. We stopped by our daughter's home to drop off some things that were left at our home the day before. We just ran in for a few minutes, gave our granddaughters a hug, and headed back out. Our son and one of his friends were working, and we dropped off some extra tools that they needed, plus some lunch! Jim and I stopped at a small café for a bite to eat on our way home. Once we were home, I fixed a plate of leftovers to take to a friend who was at work, and when I got home, Jim had a roaring fire in the fireplace! Yes, it was a very nice way to spend the day!

    I opened up my *Magnificat* this morning, and the prayer for the morning is, "Let us shout with joy at the presence of the Lord, for he comes!"

    One of my friends gave me a one-year subscription to the *Magnificat*, and I have really enjoyed reading the daily scriptures, the psalms, and stories about the saints! The following is one of today's readings:

> We urge you, brothers, admonish the idle, cheer the faint hearted, support the weak, be patient with all. See that no one returns evil for evil; rather, always seek what is good [both] for each other and for all. Rejoice always. Pray without ceasing. (1 Thessalonians 5:14–17)

> Be vigilant at all times. (Luke 21:36)

I try really hard to remember that Advent is a time of preparation, a beautiful time to reflect on the things I need to work on in my life. I pray that I will spend this Advent following the scriptures that I read each day in my *Magnificat*!

Blessings to you and yours! Bye for now.

Sharla

Preparing for Christmas with Love in My Heart!

Thursday, December 10, 2015

Good morning out there! I haven't written a post in eight days! I have a lot of catching up to do! I wanted this Advent to be a time of prayer and quiet reflection, decorating our home and baking, everything done in a peaceful and joyful setting. What was I thinking? I mean, whose life was I thinking about? It must be one of those Hallmark Christmas movies!

My life is always crazy, busy, in a wonderful, joyful, loud, boisterous, and crazy kind of way! No, there is not much time for peace and quiet reflection, but everything does get done, eventually.

As a matter of fact, I'm fixing to head out the door, but I wanted to at least start writing about my Advent adventures! I don't think *adventure* is supposed to be an adjective/adverb for Advent, but in my life, it fits! I'm going to hit Save right now, but I (hope) plan on finishing this post sometime later on today! Stay tuned. Sharla's Advent preparations for Christmas will return!

Hey, y'all, I actually made it back to my computer today! Guess what, the Morning Prayer in my *Magnificat*, which I am just now reading at 2:30 p.m., is, "Arise and Greet the Lord with Joy!"

I am a joyful person! I do try to thank the Lord for a new day right when I wake up, but sometimes, I have to stumble around a little bit, maybe drink a few sips of coffee, and then I am greeting the Lord with joy!

I really wanted to be able to write a new post each day of Advent, sharing some prayers and some scriptures. One of the reasons I have been so busy is that I have been in charge of buying the supplies for the Sack Lunch Ministry we have at our parish. I really like making sure that we have plenty of supplies. I love helping make the lunches and handing them out. People from another parish collected money and then went and bought a bunch of the travel-size hygiene items and some goodies and packaged them in large Ziploc bags. They collected a bunch of coats and caps, scarves, and gloves and delivered them to the cafeteria on Monday. Some of them stayed and helped the people look for the right size of coats and gloves after they picked up the goody bags along with their lunches. Watching those in need excitedly picking out a coat or another cap or some gloves was such an amazing blessing. I'm just so thankful to be part of this much-needed ministry. Every day this week, people have dropped off individually wrapped goodies, more scarves, hand-crocheted caps, and bottles of water. The reason I had to dash out the door this morning was because I had to go and get more groceries for the sack lunches. I was in a happy mood as I shopped at the store and loaded up the supplies in my truck. I drove to the church, and some of the ladies helped me unload the supplies and put them away. The volunteers for today already had the sack lunches ready. We have wonderful, hardworking, faithful volunteers who keep the Sack Lunch Ministry going!

I headed back home and planned what I was going to fix for lunch. My husband and son like to come home for lunch. I heated up leftover goulash and added some more green chilies and seasoning to the pan. I heated up tortillas, made lemonade, and got the tea out of the fridge. The guys came home and ate lunch while we talked about what jobs are lined up for next week. After they went back to work, I cleaned up the kitchen and then sat down to eat.

I was thinking about Advent and the Sack Lunch Ministry and taking care of my big family, and I realized something. If we do all these things with love in our hearts, then that is part of the preparation of Advent. Jesus wants us to love one another, to take care of each other.

I am going to try and slow down just a little, take some deep breaths, and carry on. This is an easy thing to remember: Pray before breakfast. Pray before bed. Read from the Book of Luke, smile at the sales clerks, and if you have time, take some baked goodies to an elderly neighbor or drop by and visit an old friend. Sing songs, bake, decorate a little each day, and drink a cup of hot cocoa. But most important of all, remember Jesus is the *reason* for the season!

Bye for now.
Sharla

December Blessings
of Life and Love

Wednesday, December 16, 2015

Good morning out there! I hope you are having a wonderful week! Today is Wednesday of the third week of Advent. In my *Magnificat*, the Prayer for the Morning is "Love and Truth Walk in God's Presence: Come, Let us adore him"!

I love this time of year. Today is my son's birthday, and next Monday is my daughter's birthday, and next Friday, we celebrate the birth of Jesus! My birthday is at the end of this month. New life, new beginnings, new blessings...December is a special month! I woke up this morning and thanked God for a beautiful new day. I looked out the window and smiled, just so happy to be able to see the beauty of God's creation! I talked to my son on the phone and wished him a happy birthday and told him that I couldn't believe he was thirty-two years old! I still remember the day he was born. It was a Friday morning, and it had snowed during the night. Jim was at my side that morning, holding my hand. We didn't know if we were having a boy or a girl, and I still remember hearing the words, "It's a boy!" A son!

When I was a little girl, my dream was to grow up and get married and have children. I wanted to have a large family and be a stay-at-home mom. I wanted to bake chocolate chip cookies for them to eat when they came home from school.

My dream came true. I love being a wife and mother and a grandmother too! Being married and having a family is a vocation, and I thank God every day for blessing me with my husband, children, and grandchildren. I put my whole heart into taking care of my family. I love to cook and bake for them. I make sure our home is always picked up and neat, although it doesn't get dusted as often as it should. I make sure the fridge and pantry are stocked. Thanks be to God we are able to do that. I'm just feeling a little nostalgic, tears of happiness with a heart full of love. I pray that all of you who take the time to read my blog posts are blessed during this special month and every day of your lives.

Blessings to you and yours!

Bye for now.

Sharla

Wednesday, December 16, 2015

This post could be the lyrics for a country and Western song! Big honkin' trailers and pickup trucks!

Hello out there! I need to add another story to my post from this morning, you know, like those promotional commercials, "But wait!" This morning, I was in a sentimental, happy mood. I wrote a post for my blog about my son's birthday and some other stuff. I made the bed, opened the blinds, turned down the heat, straightened up what needed to be straightened up, and headed out the door. I also drank two cups of coffee while all the above was going on, and then I chunked a handful of almonds and a few chocolate chips in one of the kid's Tupperware cups to take with me (one of those personalized, protein breakfast on-the-go type of thing). I drove to Sam's and picked up supplies for the Sack Lunch Ministry. This was the stock-up kind of day, not the "run in and grab some lunch meat and fruit on the go" kind of day. I don't steer those big honkin' carts very well, and the cashier had to stop me before I ran into the register stand. I smiled kind of sheepishly and thanked her. I loaded everything up into my pickup truck and headed to the church. Parishioners from St. Ambrose Catholic Church volunteered today. I was so happy to see all their smiling faces and really happy that they helped unload all those groceries! Once everything was taken care of, I dashed off to the YMCA to exercise for a little bit. Then I dashed home to eat some lunch, and as I was headed back out the door to go and buy groceries for the Ynostrosa household—because lately, that has been on the backburner—the "but wait" happened.

Jim called and said that the clutch had gone out in our son's truck. Yes, the today is his birthday, son's truck. This was the plan: Jim was going to leave work to drive over there so that our son could take Jim's truck out to a job he was trying to finish up. Jim thought that once our son's truck wasn't pulling the big honkin' trailer, it would shift gears better, and he would just head back to work in that truck, but I needed to keep my phone close by, just in case he needed me to come and get him. I drove to academy to pick up some gifts. I said some prayers on the way. I was just finishing up when my phone rang. It was Jim, and he needed me to come and pick him up. I paid for my items and drove across town. Jim and our son's truck were in a small church parking lot. I rolled down the window and said, "What's the plan?" We talked about some different ideas and decided to try and get the truck a little closer to home. Jim said that he thought he could drive the truck real slow in second gear and told me to drive behind him with my hazard lights flashing. We drove like this for all of two blocks, and Jim pulled into another parking lot. I thought we were just going to have to call a tow truck, but no, that was not Jim's idea. He told me to pull in front of the truck and he would attach a chain from my rear bumper to his front bumper and I could pull the truck. I know what you are thinking, and yes, we have done this before, more times than I care to remember! I rolled down my window, took off my sunglasses, said some more prayers, and slowly started to drive. We weren't even out of the parking lot before Jim motioned for me to stop. He parked the truck and climbed in my truck. He said that it would just be better if he waited for our son to come back when he finished his job, and they would pull the truck. I was really relieved. I drove Jim back to work, and when I started laughing, he just looked at me and shook his head. I said something like, "We are getting too old for this." And then he laughed too. I dropped him off and headed to Walmart to buy groceries for the Ynostrosa household. My basket was overflowing when I checked out. I loaded all the groceries into my truck and drove home. I received a call from my son telling me that he had just dropped off the trailer at our house and he was going to pick up Dad and they were going to pull his truck home. I said some more prayers, arrived home, and unloaded all the groceries. I was getting ready for church when I heard the guys drive up. I went outside and gave my son a hug and told him that I was sorry that this happened on his birthday, and he said that was okay, at least it didn't happen the other day when he was traveling out of town. I smiled because I'm glad that he has that "glass is half-full" type of attitude! We told him to head home. He lives about forty-five minutes away, and I knew that his wife had fixed his favorite dinner and dessert for his birthday. He told me that his sister had just called and that she was on her way with some goodies she had baked for him. We told him to go on home, that the goodies would still be good tomorrow!

Our daughter and granddaughter arrived. They brought in the gift, and then my granddaughter and I drove to the church for the La Posada celebration. It was wonderful. I'm back at home. Jim's asleep, and I am drinking a cup of sleepy time tea and sharing my adventures with y'all! In one of my earlier posts, I talked about my adventures during Advent. This one ranks pretty close to the top, right below what happened last week—driving my truck right behind Jim's truck while he pulled the stock trailer because the sheep messed up the wiring for the lights! Blessings to you and yours!

Good night.
Sharla

Come, Let Us Adore Him!

Sunday, December 20, 2015

Hello out there! A quick post before I call it a night. Today is the fourth Sunday of Advent.

We had all of our children, two sons and one daughter, their spouses, two daughters-in-law and one son-in-law, and all ten of our grandchildren with us this weekend! What a huge blessing to be able to spend time all together! We had so much fun. We laughed and played a crazy white elephant sock-exchange game. Eighteen of us in our living room. We've lived in this house, our home, for over twenty-four years. The guys barbecued, and the bigger kids played outside. We had all kinds of snacks, and the little ones played inside. I bought one of those children's nativity scenes (ages 1 to 5), and they all loved it. I placed it on their little table in the living room, and someone was always moving the figures the way they thought looked best! I took a ton of pictures and got lots of hugs and kisses! We went to the 6:00 p.m. Mass this evening, and it was wonderful; the cathedral was packed!

Jim and I have to get up really early because tomorrow is our day to spend an hour at the Adoration Chapel, so I will have to close for now.

The evening prayer in my *Magnificat* is, "Jesus Christ has opened the gates of heaven: come, let us adore him!"

I pray that you have a wonderful week and that we all slow down and enjoy this beautiful time of year.

Jesus is the reason for the season!

Bye for now.
Sharla

Baby Girls and Birthdays and the Christmas Season

Tuesday, December 22, 2015

Hello out there! Yesterday was my daughter's birthday. She is all grown up now, married with three beautiful daughters of her own. Last night, Jim and I babysat the girls while my daughter and her husband went out to eat. Their youngest daughter is our youngest grandchild, our little number 10! They were only gone for about an hour and a half, but at least they were able to eat their meal while it was still hot! I remember those days. A mom's work is never done, and more times than not, your meal goes cold by the time you get to sit down and eat! Watching my daughter take care of her family, her devotion to them, brings tears to my eyes and makes my heart swell with pride. Even though we have eight granddaughters we love so very much, our daughter will always be our baby girl no matter what!

I know that I have said this before, but I will say it again, I love being a mom! December is such a special month, and I am so thankful for my husband, children, and grandchildren! I still have so much to do before Christmas Eve, but I keep reminding myself that Christmas is a season, not just one day. The twelve days of Christmas begin on Christmas Day and go through the epiphany. I've decided that instead of stressing out, I'm going to truly celebrate the whole season! My neighbors may get baked goods on the second day of Christmas, and my Christmas cards may get mailed out on Christmas

Eve and arrive on the third day of Christmas! My plan is to spread Christmas cheer not just during the season but throughout the entire year! So if you're like me, a little behind, take a deep breath, write out a list, make yourself a cup of hot cocoa, and just sit for a minute and be blessed. Be blessed with the true beauty of what Christmas means. The true gift is love, and it can't be bought! Spend time with your loved ones. Have a special family night. Take a treat to someone who lives all alone. Call a distant relative. Just hearing your voice will be such a gift. Pray with your kids, and hug them tight! Tell your spouse you love them, and kiss their cheek! Remember to thank God for giving us His Son. Wow! Thank you, God, for giving us Your Son! Amen.

Blessings to you and yours!

Bye for now.
Sharla

Calling Them by Name

Sunday, December 27, 2015

Hello out there! The third day of Christmas, and ice is raining down! I thought it was raining really hard, and I looked outside and saw that the ground was being covered in ice! I am thankful to be inside my warm home, and I pray for those who are seeking shelter. My husband is actually out in this weather because he wanted to go and buy some cotton gloves for me to hand out at the Sack Lunch Ministry tomorrow. When Jim left, it was just misting outside. He called a minute ago and said that he already hit a slick spot and to call the kids and tell them all to stay home. It is amazing how quickly the weather can change. It looks like a winter wonderland right now. I will be glad when Jim gets back home. I hope you are all having a joyful Christmas season. I wanted to share something that happened last week at the Sack Lunch Ministry.

Another parish brought all kinds of warm clothing to hand out, even some nice winter boots. I wish you could see how the people's eyes lit up when we have extra things for them. We also handed out some more bags filled with hygiene items. Two of my granddaughters were with me last Monday, and they decorated sacks, and the older one helped hand out the sacks. A young man came in, and I called him by name. I haven't seen him in a while, and he looked surprised and said, "You remembered my name." I smiled at him and replied that I did and asked him how he was doing. My younger granddaughter who is three and a half was coloring, and I didn't realize that she was listening. A lady came in, and after she got her lunch, she was looking through the clothes. My granddaughter asked me what her name was, and I told her I didn't know. She looked at me and said, "Go and ask her." I looked down at her, and she said, "I want to know her name." I went over to the lady and smiled at her and told her that my granddaughter wanted to know what her name was. I told her my name. She smiled back and told me her name and waved at my granddaughter. I told my little one the lady's name, and she repeated it. I realized something that day, how just knowing someone's name can mean so much to them. As young as my granddaughter is, she seemed to realize that. I like to take my grandchildren with me to help out when they can. I think it helps them understand when we tell them to be grateful and thankful for all that they have. I think it also teaches them compassion and why we should always do what we are able to for others. Jim is back home, safe and sound. Thanks be to God! I pray that you are all blessed immensely during this beautiful Christmas season! There are still nine days of Christmas left. There is still time to bake cookies, send cards, make a phone call, or stop by and see an old friend!

Rejoice in the Lord always. Again, I say rejoice!

Bye for now.
Sharla

**Big Hearts and Smiles from Some
of our Faithful Volunteers!**

Sanctuary:
A Place to Worship
A Safe Place to Rest

Hello out there! I hope each day of this New Year has been and will continue to be wonderful! Something happened this week that stopped me in my tracks, brought tears to my eyes, and made compassion fill up in my heart so fast I had to catch my breath. I will tell you a condensed version of the story up until the important part.

Tuesday, January 5, 2016

I went to Sam's to buy supplies for the Sack Lunch Ministry and drove back to church, where Muriel and I unloaded the supplies and stocked the fridge and the pantry.

I decided to go into the cathedral to pray before I left. I walked into the church, the vestibule, and just stood for a minute. It is always so quiet and peaceful during the day. The lights on the Christmas tree were plugged in, and there was a little bit of light coming through the stained glass windows, but it was a cloudy day, so the sanctuary was only dimly lit. I stopped to pray at the shrine of Our Lady of Guadalupe, and then I walked further into the sanctuary and filled up my little container with holy water. I walked up to the tabernacle and knelt down to pray. It was so quiet in there, and when I stood up to leave, something caught my eye. I saw something blue on the pew in front of the altar. I walked toward it, looked down, and immediately stood still. A homeless man was sound asleep on the pew, wrapped up in a sleeping bag, his feet clad in worn tennis shoes and sticking out. He had two bags, one on the floor and one next to his head. He was sound asleep, snoring peacefully, and my hand reached out to touch him just to pat his shoulder, but I stopped because I didn't want to wake or startle him, so I made the sign of the cross over him and said a quiet little prayer for him. I stood there for a moment, so overcome with this heartbreaking yet beautiful picture, thinking about how the sanctuary where we worship was a different type of sanctuary for him. He felt safe there; his tired body was able to sleep peacefully because he knew he would be safe. I walked over to the kitchen and grabbed some crackers, some nuts, some fruit, and a bottle of water and walked back to the sanctuary, planning to quietly leave the food by his other things, but he was already gone. I walked around the church looking for him. I drove around the block, but he was gone.

Wednesday, January 6, 2016

I was helping Miss Rose (her name is Rosa, but we call her Miss Rose), and I told her about the man. She told me that he had come in on Tuesday for a sack lunch. He didn't have a shirt on under his thin coat, so she went to the pantry where we keep some extra things during the cold months to help those who live on the streets. She took out a new sleeping bag that had been donated from another Catholic parish (St. Ambrose) and gave him that along with some warm cotton gloves. She said that he sat in the cafeteria and ate, and when he was through, he asked if he could have another sandwich, and they gave him another one. Most people take their lunches with them, but they are always welcome to sit and eat in the cafeteria if they want to.

Another lady and I went into the pantry and dug through the bags with gloves and socks, and we found a warm sweatshirt; it was brand new. We took the sweatshirt and two pairs of socks and placed them close by so that if he came back, they could put the clothes in another sack for him. He didn't show up for lunch on Wednesday.

Thursday, January 7, 2016

Although the sun was shining, the wind made it really chilly, especially if you have to be outside. There were four of us handing out lunches that day. We all talked about how thankful we were for this ministry that helps so many. We wondered if the man will come back. About 12:30 p.m., he limped in, got his lunch, and sat down to eat. I got the sweatshirt and two pair of socks, put them in a bag, and took them to him. He smiled and thanked us. I went into the pantry and once again filled a bag with some crackers, some nuts, some fruit, and another bottle of water. I took it to him, and he smiled and told us that we were too sweet. I told him that we were happy to do this for him. He thanked us and left. We closed up for the day, but the next day, we once again handed out lunches to those in need. This ministry blesses my heart as much as the food fills their hungry stomachs.

I knew on the way home that I had to write a post about this man, this story, so when I got home, I fixed something quick to eat and headed to my office.

I got out my big old *Random House College Dictionary* and looked up the word *sanctuary*. These are some of the different definitions:

1. A sacred or holy place
2. Judaism, a. the biblical tabernacle or the temple in Jerusalem b. The holy of holies of these places of worship
3. An especially holy place in a temple or church
4. The part of a church around the altar; the chancel

5. A church or other sacred place formerly providing refuge of asylum.

There are some more definitions, but I mainly wanted to point out the fifth. I'm so thankful that the man who was sleeping in the front pew of the sanctuary in our cathedral parish found the sanctuary he was seeking. I am going to close with the refrain from one of my favorite hymns. If you have read very many of my posts, you will recognize it.

"We are many parts, we are all one body, and the gifts we have we are given to share. May the Spirit of love make us one indeed; one, the love that we share, one, our hope in despair, one the cross that we bear."

Bye for now.
Sharla

You Might Be Catholic If… You Just Took Your Nativity Scene Down!

Friday, January 15, 2016

Hello out there! The sun is shining, and it is a beautiful day! I just brought my outside nativity scene in yesterday. I carefully carried in the statues of Mother Mary, St. Joseph, Baby Jesus, and the manger. I set them up in the living room just like they were outside. I brought in the statues of the lambs, the donkey, the steer, the star, and the small angel. This is a big nativity scene. The statue of Joseph is three and a half feet tall, to give you an idea of the size. I knew I wouldn't be able to put everything up in the boxes until today, so I made sure the nativity scene was set up in the living room, out of the way. Jim came home and said, "I see you've moved the holy family inside," and I laughed and promised I would put them up soon! This morning, I left early to pick up supplies for the Sack Lunch Ministry. I drove to the church and put all the supplies away while Ms. Rose was making the sandwiches. The other volunteers showed up, and Janice and I sat down to write out an article for the church bulletin, thanking everyone for all the coats, caps, socks, gloves, blankets, toiletries, and food items that were donated to the Sack Lunch Ministry over the Christmas season. My daughter and two of my granddaughters stopped by to visit, and then we ran over to the noon Mass. We were running a few minutes late, but we made it! Jim and our son were already there. They work together. We have a family business, and they decided to go to Mass since I would already be there helping with the lunches. I always love it when we are at Mass together!

I ran some errands and came home. I fixed a quick snack for lunch, ate, and looked at my nativity scene. I knew it was time to put it away. I got a damp cloth and carefully wiped each statue and put them in their designated boxes and placed the boxes in my "Christmas closet." I prayed as I put my nativity scene away. I prayed for families everywhere. I prayed for moms, I prayed for dads, and I prayed for the babies and children of all ages.

I hope you all have a wonderful, safe weekend! Hug your spouse, hug your kids, and thank the Good Lord for your blessings! I am trying to keep the spirit of Christmas in my heart the whole year through! Blessings, blessings, blessings to you! Bye for now.

Sharla

Life Is a Blessing!

Monday, February 1, 2016

Hello out there! It is a beautiful day! How are y'all doing? I need to write a long post to share everything that has been going on over the last twelve days! The last post I wrote was on January 19! I can't believe it has been that long! I will write a quick (ha-ha) summary.

Friday, January, 22, 2016.

The horrible anniversary of Roe v. Wade.

Pro-Life Rosary in the courtyard at Sacred Heart at 4:30 p.m., followed by Mass in the cathedral at Sacred Heart. Bishop Michael Sis was the celebrant and his homily was wonderful. Drove home and loaded up an overnight bag in the truck, and Jim and I headed to Austin! We arrived at our hotel in South Austin about 11:00 p.m. (I have to go and get ready for the 6:00 p.m. Mass right now. I will finish with my summary tomorrow morning, Lord willing!)

Saturday, January 23, 2016

Texas Rally for Life in Austin and Texas Catholic Pro-Life Day

Pro-Life Rosary and Vigil in front of the Planned Parenthood on Ben White Blvd. from 7 a.m. to 8:30 a.m.

Mass of Thanksgiving for the Gift of Human Life at St. Vincent de Paul Parish, celebrated by Bishop Vasquez at 10:00 a.m. The Mass was beautiful! The sanctuary was packed, standing room only! Families and youth groups from all across Texas filled the pews! The choir was angelic: the St. Vincent de Paul children's choir, Holy Family Catholic School choir, and St. Dominic Savio Catholic High School choir! It was very uplifting to be with so many other pro-life people. Everything was so organized, even the parking!

The pro-life march to the courthouse was really exciting. There were so many people. It was amazing! Banners and pro-life signs. So many young people: moms and dads, babies, toddlers, teens, grandparents!

The rally at the courthouse was great. The speakers were excellent, and the music was too! A really awesome day!

Jim and I drove home on Sunday and went to Mass at 6:00 p.m. Monday morning, we went to Adoration from 5:00 a.m. to 6:00 a.m., and then the regular work week began. I picked up supplies for the Sack Lunch Ministry on Tuesday and worked on tax stuff for our family business the rest of the week. I also started signing people up for the 40 Days for Life Spring Campaign, which begins next week!

Saturday, January 30, 2016

My oldest grandchild turned ten today! My oldest grandchild, who is also my oldest grandson, turned ten on Saturday! Where does the time go? He is almost as tall as me. He has a big heart, a beautiful smile, and is a really awesome big brother and an all-around great kid! Yes, I am a little partial, but he is a blessing to us all! His birthday party was at their home. They live out in the country, a perfect party for a boy! BB gun target shooting. Yes, there was plenty of supervision! Chase, hide, and go seek, rock chunking, you name it! They all had a great time! Well, I have a lot to accomplish today, so I better close for now. I hope you all have a wonderful week. Thank you for taking the time to read my blog.

Blessings and peace,
Sharla

The Greatest of
These Is Love!

Wednesday, February 3, 2016

Good morning out there! The Spring 40 Days for Life Campaign begins next Wednesday! So much to do! I love kids! I just have to share some of the things that have happened the last couple of days. In my previous post, I told y'all all about my oldest grandchild's tenth birthday party and how much fun it was. I can't believe he is already ten. Life just goes by too fast!

I teach fourth grade CCD classes at my parish on Monday nights. We have been learning the Ten Commandments and the Corporal Works of Mercy. One of the moms gave me a sack full of scapulars, crosses, prayers cards, etc., for me to hand out in class. I poured everything out on the table and told them that they could each pick something out after they told me one of the commandments or the works of mercy. I called on them one by one. When they called out the answer, I wrote it on the board, and then they got to pick one of the items. They were all so excited, and each child was able to answer correctly. One of the young men said, "Do not take the Lord's name in vain." Then he asked me if I would explain exactly what that meant again. I explained it and some other questions that came up. These children are nine and ten years old. They love to learn and are so inquisitive.

My three-and-a-half-year-old granddaughter was in class with us. She wanted to answer a question also. I asked her what she thought one of the answers was, and she shouted out, "Pray for the babies!" Isn't that great? No, that is not one of the Ten Commandments or one of The Corporal Works of Mercy, but as young as she is, she understood that we were talking about serious things, and she gave a serious answer! She picked a prize, and that answer went on the board also. Kids do listen, even when you don't think they are. They are like little sponges just soaking it all in. I love being part of their lives! I try to cram everything I can into that one hour and fifteen minutes I have with them on Monday nights. They love to learn, and I love to learn with them!

Yesterday, twenty-five students from Angelo Catholic School helped us at the Sack Lunch Ministry. They made the sandwiches, put everything in the sacks, and handed them out. They also decorated a *bunch* of sacks for us! We loved having them help us, and we hope they will come back soon!

I hope you all have a great day! Blessings,
Sharla

Corporal Works of Mercy:

- To feed the hungry
- To give drink to the thirsty
- To clothe the naked
- To welcome the stranger
- To heal the sick
- To visit the imprisoned
- To bury the dead

Beautiful Prayer from Pope Saint John Paul II

Friday, February 5, 2016

Good morning out there! I just want to share a prayer that was in our parish bulletin a couple of weeks ago.

Day of Prayer for the Legal Protection of Unborn Children

"A great prayer for life is urgently needed,
a prayer which will rise up throughout the world.
Through special initiatives and in daily prayer,
may an impassioned plea rise to God,
the Creator and lover of life, from every Christian community,
from every group and association,
from every family and from the heart of every believer."
Pope Saint John Paul II

Blessings and peace,
Sharla

Please Say a Little Prayer for Me!

Tuesday, February 9, 2016

Good morning! Good morning! Hello out there! I've been awake since 4:00 a.m. The Fat Tuesday Pancake Dinner Kick-Off Rally is tonight! Writing out my list and checking it twice! I'm thinking six cans of whipping cream for the pancakes will be enough. Yes, we are having syrup also. I just thought the kids might like some whipping cream too! I have the *Horton Hears a Who* movie. I need someone to please set up the movie projector thingy in the gym for me. (Thank You!) We have plenty of tables in the cafeteria, but I wanted to set up some table in the gym for the kids while they are watching the movie (dinner and a movie)!

I'm picking up table cloths for the tables we set up in the gym. I think about six of them. Jim will be there to help set up! I think balloons hanging up on the gates in the courtyard will be a nice touch! A welcoming entrance! Y'all come and eat pancakes and sign-up to pray in the courtyard during the 40 Days for Life!

I probably won't have much time to post in the next couple of days, so I just wanted to say hello and tell y'all to have a great week! I pray that all of you who read this are safe and warm and know how very much God loves you! I'm always amazed and humbled when I see that people from different countries take the time to read my blog. Thank you, and God bless you all!

I'm closing with a quote from Dr. Seuss, "And even if you can't see themor hear them at all…A person's a person no matter how small!"

Bye for now.
Sharla

My conversation with Jim as he is heading out the door.

"–Now, Sharla, be careful when you are driving. I know how you are when you have so much going on. Pay attention to the road!" I laughed and said for him to say a prayer and ask St. Raphael to watch out for me. "I already did, and St. Raphael told me that he does the best he can but you are crazy!" I laughed some more, gave him a kiss, and reminded him that I needed help setting up the tables! I love my husband! Look out, world! Here I come!

In My Father's Courtyard

Thursday, February 11, 2016

Good morning out there! The kick-off rally for the 40 Days for Life was great! Fat Tuesday Pancake Dinner with all kinds of toppings: blueberries, strawberries, whipping cream, sprinkles, and of course butter and syrup. We even had a request for peanut butter, and that was available also! Sausage links or ham was served up on the side!

Day 1 of our peaceful, prayerful vigil was amazing. So many people showed up to pray! I had gone into the kitchen to help with the Sack Lunch Ministry, and then I walked back through the hall towards the courtyard. I wanted to make sure that someone was still out there. I stopped just as I reached the doors and looked through the glass. Tears welled up in my eyes, and I started singing this song that came upon my heart.

> In my Father's courtyard, this is what I see,
> faithful smiling people looking back at me.

> In my Father's courtyard, faith and love abound.
> In my Father's courtyard, prayers go round and round.

> In my Father's courtyard, this is what I see,
> prayerful wonderful people looking back at me.

In my Father's courtyard, you'll feel His healing peace.

In my Father's courtyard is where I long to be.

God is so good! I feel so blessed! I'm headed to the courtyard. Come and join me! Be blessed!

Bye for now.

Sharla

In Our Father's Courtyard, This Is What You'll See!

Wednesday, February 17, 2016

Good morning out there! The last week has been wonderful! Just a quick post to share some uplifting news from the courtyard!

Friday, February 12, 2016

There were people praying in the courtyard all throughout the day! I stopped by before I went to the noon Mass, and this is what I saw: four amazing ladies praying the rosary together, another awesome lady praying by herself, a homeless man sitting on a bench eating his lunch that he had just received from our Sack Lunch Ministry, and another faithful man, my friend, and a member of the Knights of Columbus, painting the benches in the courtyard! I love the joy and fellowship that absolutely grabs you when you walk into the courtyard!

Friday evening, I stopped back by, and this is what I saw: a beautiful devoted married couple and another very faithful prayer warrior sitting at the picnic table eating dinner together. A fish fry was going on in the cafeteria, a fundraiser for the youth trips, and the couple bought dinner for the three of them! I walked up and gave them all a hug! We visited for a little while, and Mrs. Cain, my faithful prayer warrior, told me that she was at home crocheting little baby caps for the moms who go to the pregnancy help center. She decided that since she was praying while she was crocheting, she'd just come to the courtyard and pray and crochet there! Then she was blessed with a wonderful fish dinner! Don't you just love that?

I have more to share, but it will have to be tomorrow! Blessings! Blessings to you and yours!

Bye for now.
Sharla

Trimming trees in the courtyard

Happy Memories, Tears, Love, and Yellow Yarn!

Thursday, February 25, 2016

Good morning out there! A quick post before I head to the courtyard! Today is day 16 of the 40 Days for Life Campaign! I wish that everyone who reads this blog could spend just one hour in the courtyard! I love being out there! Every day brings new blessings! I have to share what happened last Friday. One of my sweetest prayer warriors is Mrs. Cain. She is in her eighties and is just an absolute joy to be around. She brings her crochet hooks and yarn with her and prays and crochets! She makes the cutest little caps for newborn babies, and then she donates them to our local pregnancy help center.

I don't know how to crochet. My mom tried to teach me the summer before she passed away from cancer. I remember sitting by her on our couch—I was twelve—and she was making an afghan for me. The colors were bright yellow and orange. I still have it! My grandmother was making an afghan for my brother. It was green and white. My mom taught me the basics. After she died, I never tried to crochet again until last Friday afternoon. I showed up at the courtyard at about 1:30 p.m. Mrs. Cain was praying and crocheting! I sat down next to her and gave her a big hug! She handed me a crochet hook and gave me some bright yellow yarn. She told me to just start making a chain like I remembered. After a while, she showed me how to make a circle and start connecting the rows. We laughed and visited, and before we knew it, over three hours had passed. Other people praying in the courtyard stopped by to visit with us as they were about to leave. It was a wonderful day, and it brought back a lot of wonderful memories. The baby cap I was supposed to be making ended up being a big bright yellow doily! Mrs. Cain was so proud of me, and she told me that we would practice some more on another day out in the courtyard. I enjoyed the day so much, and even though my mom has been gone for many years, just writing about this brings tears to my eyes. I will always miss her!

I hope you all have a wonderful day. I'm headed to the courtyard, and I will pop in at the Sack Lunch Ministry, another place near and dear to my heart! God bless you all! Hug your spouse, hug your kids, and call your mama and your dad if you are still blessed to have them here with you! Every day of our life is a gift!

I try to make sure that I do something each day to give as a gift back to God! A smile goes a long way, hugs are great, your children are precious, and please always pray for your spouse!

A wedding is a day. A marriage is a lifetime and takes love and prayers, patience and kindness, and, most of all, dependence on God!

Blessings to you and yours.

Sharla

In Loving Memory of My Parents
Arthur and Marty Nelson

Best Friends Forever!

40 Days for Life Continues
Please Join Us!

Sunday, March 6, 2016

Hello out there! It is almost 11:00 p.m. on Sunday night, and I am wide awake! Jim and I have to be at the Adoration Chapel early tomorrow morning, and I should already be asleep! Oh well, since I'm not, I will use my time wisely and tell y'all what has been going on during the 40 Days for Life in the courtyard! It is hard to believe that there are only two weeks left in this campaign. I just sent out another invite to everyone on Facebook about stopping by the courtyard and praying during the next two weeks. I also attached a bunch of great pictures of people and children (my grandchildren) who have been out in the courtyard. It really is a wonderful way to spend time with your family. My whole family is involved. I have pictures of the grandkids watering the plants, trimming the bushes, drawing with sidewalk chalk, praying, making posters, signing people up before the campaign begins, and having fun at all the kick-off rallies! Thank goodness for my husband. He does so much to help me get ready for the campaigns, and he is really great during the campaigns. Forty days is a long time, and I am crazier than usual. The laundry stacks up. The housecleaning is hit and miss as I run out the door, and he washes a lot of dishes! He also helps set things up, and he just fabricated (he's a welder) a beautiful iron frame for the canvas picture of Our Lady of Guadalupe. He finished it yesterday, and then he picked it back up today and made some minor modifications to it (at my request). I know, I know, he is awesome! We are going to place it back in the courtyard early tomorrow morning after we leave the Adoration Chapel. I also have to tell you about all the faithful, wonderful people who come and pray. Every day is a blessing. I love driving up and seeing people praying; some in groups, some by themselves. There are three different rosary groups that come and pray the Pro-Life Rosary on different days! My friend, Candi, who is also my official right hand and co-coordinator, has been amazing! She has been such a blessing to me and to our courtyard campaign! She arrives early and sets things up, helps me plan the rallies, and purchase the supplies. She is always smiling and full of the Holy Spirit! She remembers the things I forget, and everyone loves her!

We have so much fun when we go to the store, and I love bouncing ideas back and forth with her. She is a great friend and a very faithful and devoted prayer warrior! She and I decorated a prayer request box this past Friday. We are going to place it on the table with the sign-in sheet and the prayer books. We have some note cards for those who want to fill out a prayer request and drop it in the box.

The tenth grade confirmation class had a retreat at Sacred Heart yesterday. They wrote wonderful, colorful pro-life messages all over the concrete slab in and around the courtyard with sidewalk chalk. I saw their artwork this morning. My heartfelt so full, and I thanked God for their parents and teachers.

This is our fourth 40 Days for Life Campaign in the courtyard at Sacred Heart. Each campaign has been unique and special in its own way. Different blessings and more blessings each time. The fellowship in the courtyard really warms your heart. Peace and quiet, a shoulder to lean on, an ear to listen, and warm hugs are just a few of the added joys I have experienced! I better close for now. I hope you all have a wonderful week. Please remember to pray for the unborn and their families from wherever you are. I am going to close with the sing-song poem I wrote during the first couple of days during this campaign. I just thought of another verse, "In my Father's courtyard, children laugh and play, drawing on the sidewalk as their parents pray. In my Father's courtyard, families can be found. In my Father's courtyard, prayers go round and round."

Peace and Blessings to You and Yours All across the World!

Thursday, March 10, 2016

Hello out there! I just wanted to share something that really touched my heart this morning when I was looking at the stat section of my blog. When I started this blog almost two years ago, I wasn't even on FB yet. I just had so much that was in my heart and on my mind that I wanted to say and to share. I hoped this blog would help people. I wanted my posts to somehow make a difference. This morning, I noticed that people from other countries have been reading my blog. Besides the United States, people from Russia, Germany, Ukraine and Syria, Italy, Romania, Australia, Poland, Sweden, and Mexico have read some of my posts, and I am amazed and very humbled.

It just brought tears to my eyes. I pray that my posts bring a smile to your face, maybe tears to your eyes, even make you laugh sometimes. Maybe my posts help some of you look at things in a different way. I pray that my posts touch your hearts. Thank you for taking the time to include my blog in your lives. I will keep you and your families and your countries in my prayers. God bless you all.

I noticed something else that grabbed my heart this morning. My daughter wrote a comment on the previous post I wrote, and once again, the tears started. I always pray that God will help me be a light for my family, a good example, and to teach them to stand up for what you believe in. Someday, I hope that my grandchildren will look back on these blog posts and laugh at all our fun family gatherings. I pray they will remember how very much I love them. I pray that they will see how my faith in God leads me in everything that I do.

I'm feeling very sentimental today. I'm sure you have realized that by now. Tomorrow or in the next couple of days, I'm sure something crazy will happen, and I will be writing another one of my "country song, redneck posts," so until then, may your day be full of blessings and your heart full of song.

Bye for now.

Sharla

Candles and Prayers

Monday, March 14, 2016

Hello out there! It is an absolutely gorgeous day! I try to always be thankful and to remember that compared to many others, I have no reason to ever complain about anything!

After Mass last night, Jim gave me some money and asked me to buy three candles for us to bring home. I bought the candles. Our priest blessed them for me, and then I stopped in the courtyard, said a quick prayer, and gathered up the prayer books and 40 Days for Life sign-in sheet.

On the way home, I asked Jim who we were going to light the candles for and lift up with extra prayers this week. Jim had read the Sunday paper earlier in the day. I had not read it yet. He told me about the chemical warfare that was going on and the people who were wounded and killed.

I just felt sick to my stomach as he told me the news. He said one candle is for the innocent people in the countries where the chemical warfare broke out, the second candle is for some dear friends who are going through a lot, and the third candle is for our grandchildren.

Right before we went to bed, Jim lit all three candles. We put them on top of the stove, a safe place for them to burn at night. (Or just light the candles and keep them lit when you are at home and awake.) We stood there in the kitchen next to the stove and prayed. As we prayed, I began to cry. I just felt so helpless about what was going on in the other countries. When we finished praying, we talked about how important it is to pray for others. My heart felt a little lighter as we went to bed. When the alarm went off at 4:00 a.m. this morning, I put the pillow over my head. Jim was the first one up—he always is—and when he was almost ready he said, "Sharla, it's time to get up. We have to go to Adoration, and we don't need to be in a hurry."

I stuck one of my legs out of the covers and thought to myself, "Maybe I'll just sit this one out," and then I said to myself, "That is exactly what the devil wants me to do!" I threw back the covers and quickly got ready. Jim brought me a cup of coffee. He knows me so well! We arrived at the Adoration Chapel right on time. We spent a very peaceful and prayerful hour, and then we headed home. On the way home, I told Jim how I almost stayed in bed this morning, and he said in a laughing and shocked voice, "You need to say three Our Fathers for that!" I laughed and said, "No, I do not because I did not stay in bed. I went to adoration!" And I'm sure glad I did! Going to the Adoration Chapel on Monday mornings is a great way to start the week off right!

Back to the reality of what is going on in the world right now, we need to pray, and we need to pray hard for families all across the world. Last week, I posted the Divine Mercy Chaplet on my blog, a wonderful prayer for the whole world. May God bless you and keep you safe wherever you are.

Bye for now.
Sharla

Love Is Patient, Love Is Kind, and Prayer Is A Must!

Friday, March 18, 2016

Good morning out there! The courtyard has been so full of life this week! Every day in the courtyard brings a different kind of blessing. Monday night, there were people in the courtyard from five different parishes praying for an end to abortion. The Knights of Columbus Council from the Olfen, Rowena, Ballinger and Miles area drove into town to pray the Pro-Life Rosary and then headed back to where they have their meetings. It probably took thirty-five minutes or so to drive in, and I really appreciate their devotion and effort! (A couple of their wives were with them too!)

Members of the St. Philomena Rosary group from St. Mary's and a married couple from Sacred Heart were all praying in the courtyard. It was wonderful to see so many people praying at once.

Tuesday morning, I went to the courtyard and spent a couple of hours. My friend and co-coordinator, Candi, was still there when I showed up. She arrives early and sets everything up and stays to pray her daily devotions. We always have a quick visit and sometimes not so quick before she leaves! We both agree on how special the prayers in the courtyard are and the blessings of peace we receive. My daughter and her three girls (three of my granddaughters) came to pray. The girls and I went inside to visit everyone at the Sack Lunch Ministry and then walked over to the cathedral to say a prayer while their mom was praying in the courtyard. Then the girls drew pictures with the sidewalk chalk. The oldest was also busy helping me with the two younger ones! They also said some prayers! My daughter was praying in one area, another lady was praying across from her, and the girls were out in the middle. I was sitting on a bench visiting with a man who had picked up a lunch and wanted some information about Mass times. I grabbed one of the daily devotionals we had on the table and gave it to him. We walked over to the church and went into the vestibule. It had been a while since he had been inside a Catholic Church, and he was very moved. I gave him a bulletin that lists the Mass schedule. He was very thankful and seemed a bit happier when he left.

Wednesday was another beautiful day in the courtyard. The weather was perfect! The sun was shining, there was a very slight breeze, and it was just a gorgeous day! Little sparrows and doves were flying in and out of the trees, hop-hopping on the concrete, and tweet-tweeting their joyful songs! Several people stopped by the picnic table where we have the sign-in sheet, the prayer books, rosaries, daily devotions, and brochures. They asked questions and visited and took some of the brochures and devotions with them. It was one of those days I could have stayed all day! I left at about 2:30 p.m. and went to the grocery store. I was buying groceries for a dinner I was going to cook that evening for some friends who were coming over. My husband and I are sponsors for a couple who want to get married in the church. We have known this young couple for years. We shared a wonderful meal and discussed marriage preparation and talked about our own marriage. It was a wonderful evening, and we were very happy to spend time with this sweet couple. They know that we are here for them and we will meet with them again. I always say, "A wedding is a day. A marriage is a lifetime," and if you want to have good marriage, it takes work! Communication is very important. You can't read each other's minds, so talk! God must be number one in your marriage. Pray together, pray for each other, and attend Mass as a family. Pray when you wake up, thank the Lord for a new day, and ask for His help throughout the day. Pray before meals. Always thank God for the food you have to eat, and ask Him to be with those who don't. Pray before you go to sleep! Hold hands, hug, laugh, and be quick to forgive! Put down the phones! Talk to each other, and make sure your friends are on the same path you are! Remember to say "Thank you," and "Please," and "You're welcome" to each other.

Love is patient. Love is kind! Marriage is awesome!

I'll have to tell y'all about the Chrism Mass and the blessings in the courtyard from Thursday later!

Have a super great day, a day full of blessings!

Bye for now.

Sharla

A Prayer for the Whole World

"Dear God, please watch over all these countries where war has broken out. Please, God, protect the innocent people and their families. Please, God, open their government's eyes to the devastation that war is causing. Please, God, guide their leaders to a peaceful solution. Thank you, God, for our many blessings. Please be with all those who are in need. Please, God, show us, guide us, on how we can best help others. You created us all. Please help us to love our neighbor, care for one another, and to pray for those who seek a better life. In Jesus's name I pray, dear Lord, amen."

Holy Week, Easter Sunday, Birthday Blessings: Faith and Family!

Wednesday, March 30, 2016

Hello out there! I hope you all felt God's grace and love during Holy Week! It was a very busy but wonderful week for us. Jim and I went to the Holy Thursday Mass, the Good Friday service, and the Easter Vigil. Each night was so special. I loved it all. The scriptures, homilies, music, atmosphere, and the smell of incense are just a few of the memorable blessings of Holy Week. Receiving the Eucharist during Communion and then going to Eucharistic Adoration after the Holy Thursday Mass were such a blessing it brought tears to my eyes. The Good Friday service is always a very emotional and sobering experience. When we walked into the cathedral sanctuary, it was dimly lit, and all the statues were covered, the tabernacle doors were open, and it was so quiet. The reality of Jesus dying on the cross just hits you. There is no opening hymn because the service starts right where it left off from Holy Thursday. The Easter Vigil begins in the courtyard where the Easter candle is lit from the flames of the fire, and then we process into the sanctuary, and everyone's candles are then lit. The music is angelic, and the readings are powerful. I was blessed to be asked to read the sixth reading (Baruch 3:9–15,32 to 4:4). I loved reading the emotional verses of scripture from the

Prophet Baruch. The people who have been taking the RCIA classes received their sacraments during the vigil. Some received all three sacraments: baptism, first Holy Communion, and confirmation.

Others received their first Holy Communion and confirmation. There were a few that had been baptized and had made their first Holy Communion but had never been confirmed, so they received their confirmation.

The Easter Vigil always brings back wonderful memories for me because I received my first Holy Communion and was confirmed in 1987 in the very same sanctuary, the Cathedral Church of the Sacred Heart.

The Easter Vigil is a very long Mass, about 3.5 hours, and it is an incredible, peace-filled, emotionally moving experience.

Easter Sunday was a beautiful "He is risen, is risen, alleluia" day!

I put a spiral sliced ham in the oven, made a pistachio pudding, pineapple cool-whip salad, also known as the green stuff, and put it in the fridge. Our centerpiece was rice krispies shaped as nests filled with green-colored coconut and jelly beans. I put the nests in the middle of my grandma's old depression glass platter and placed green-colored coconut grass, whopper eggs, and chicken peeps all around the nests. I had soaked a pot of pinto beans the night before, and they were cooking on top of the stove. Jim was busy cleaning up the yard for the Easter egg hunt, and he also helped clean up the house. I popped a casserole dish of red potatoes in the oven and pulled the frozen rolls from the freezer. My daughter and daughter-in-law brought the desserts and other sides.

We had three stages for this special day:

1. Say grace and eat lunch
2. Hide and hunt Easter eggs
3. Birthday party. Our youngest grandchild turned one year old on Easter Sunday! She had a great day!

It was about 7:00 p.m. by the time everyone had left. A super great day, and we were super tired!

Easter Monday began with our usual early morning hour at the Adoration Chapel, a great way to start the week!

I have to go and fix some supper now, but I just had to write this post and say hello to y'all. I'll write more later on.

Bye for now.
Sharla

Unexpected Blessings,
Finding God Everywhere!

Saturday, April 9, 2016

Hello out there! How has your week been? I'm so happy that I finally have time to sit down and write a post. It has been ten days since I wrote my last one. I think I will do a time line to catch y'all up on everything.

On Thursday, March 31, Jim and I headed out of town. We were going to see our oldest son and his family in the Houston area on Friday, April 1. We decided to take off a day early and just take our time and stop here and there and everywhere! We were supposed to leave early on Thursday morning. The early part didn't happen. We left around 11:00 a.m. I only had to run back into the house twice to grab the things I forgot. We weren't even out of the driveway yet, so it wasn't a big deal. When Jim asked me if I was sure I had everything, I smiled and said, "Yes, I think so." Then I told him to drive kind of slow as we were going down the street so that I could go over everything we brought just in case we had to turn around. I did get a look from him on that comment. After a few minutes, I said, "We're good. Let's say a prayer and speed it up!" Jim always says that patience is a virtue, and it is not one of the virtues that he has. After being married to me for almost thirty-three years, I think Jim has definitely earned the patience virtue!

We do have a good time when we are able to travel out of town. We take our time and stop whenever we see something interesting or if we just want to take another look. We are known to whip U-turns, but only on country roads when there isn't much traffic. We stopped at a little town southeast of Temple, TX, to visit a sweet couple who moved away from San Angelo years ago. They have always been like a second set of parents to Jim, and they are special to me also! We stayed a couple of hours and then continued on our way. We pulled into Bryan/College Station just as the sun was going down. We were trying to find a place to stay and took a wrong turn. Then all of a sudden, I cried out, "Look, St. Anthony's Catholic Church! He found us!" Jim found a place to park, and we got out and walked around. You will not believe what we found. They have a beautiful rosary garden dedicated to the unborn. It is called St. Anthony's Walking Rosary, and the sign says that it was dedicated and blessed on December 8, 2006, as a memorial for the victims of abortion in our community and in our world. My eyes filled with tears, and I began to cry as I read all the names of the groups and people who contributed to the garden. I told Jim how much God knows our hearts and how amazing it is that St. Anthony helped us find our way to this special place. We walked along the stepping stones of the rosary for a few minutes, and then we checked the Mass schedule and drove off to find a hotel. The next morning, we woke up early and drove back to St. Anthony's Church for the 7:15 a.m. Mass. It was overcast, and a heavy mist was falling as we parked and dashed to the prayer chapel. Mass was wonderful, and afterward, we talked to some of the parishioners. Some people were cleaning the large church sanctuary, and they let us go in and look around. It is a beautiful old Catholic Church. Another lady stopped by and told us that we should go over to St. Joseph's Catholic Church for the 8:15 a.m. Mass with the school children. Jim and I finished looking at the church, and when we walked outside, that same lady was waiting in her vehicle for us to follow her. We went to Mass at St. Joseph's and really enjoyed seeing all the school children. The sanctuary was full of families. I love seeing the mothers and fathers and all the little ones! Jim and I felt so blessed. What an awesome way to begin our Friday morning. After Mass, we met some more people, and we were introduced to the priest. While Jim and I were looking at the beautiful Old Testament story-telling stained-glass windows, a lady walked up and started talking to us. Her name is Ruth, and she is the sweetest woman. She led us through the doors to the Adoration Chapel and told us to sign in.

As Jim and I were kneeling to say our prayers, she brought us three rosaries and some reading material to take with us. Ruth told us that one rosary was for our vehicle and the other two were for us. She hugged us, and then she was gone. Jim and I stayed for a little while and prayed. Tears kept streaming down my face. I could feel the Holy Spirit right there with us. When Jim and I got into the truck, I immediately hung up one of the rosaries on our rearview mirror. We went back to the hotel, had some breakfast, packed, and checked out. We had only been gone from home a little over twenty-four hours and were so humbled at the blessings we had received. I just kept thinking about one of my favorite hymns, "Lead Me, Lord." I sing the refrain from it a lot.

"Lead me, Lord. Lead me, Lord, by the light of truth, to seek and to find the narrow way. Be my way. Be my truth. Be my life, my Lord, and lead me, Lord, today."

We traveled toward our oldest son's home. We stopped at a neat store on the side of the highway. There was every kind of concrete statue you could imagine and a bunch of other stuff too! Jim took a picture of me next to a life-size painted statue of a lion. I wanted to take a picture of him by a big ape, but he wouldn't cooperate! We journeyed on, stopped at a barbecue place and ate, and then drove on to our destination. We checked in at our hotel, freshened up, and drove over to our son's home. Our granddaughters ran out to greet us right as we drove up. Hugs and more hugs, kisses too, and then we all loaded up and headed to the field where our younger granddaughter was having her first softball scrimmage. She is seven, and she is the catcher; our son is the coach. We enjoyed the game. They both did a great job! We found a place to eat dinner, and then we called it a night! The next day was going to start early, and we all needed a good night's rest! I will have to finish telling about the rest of our trip in the next day or two! I've been running back and forth fixing dinner and washing dishes while I wrote this post! The cornbread is almost ready, and the goulash is simmering! Have a wonderful evening. God bless you all wherever you are!

Bye for now.

Sharla

Blessings from Our Journey: Family, Historic Catholic Church, and a Refuge!

Tuesday, April 12, 2016

Good morning! Good morning! It is a beautiful day! Hello out there! I hope your week is going well! My last post was about the wonderful blessings that happened during the first couple of days of our trip. Today, I want to tell you about some more of our neat experiences. I ended my last post with Friday evening, April 1.

Saturday morning, we woke up early and headed to the baseball/softball complex. It was opening day, and they were having a small parade. The teams and their coaches walked from the school to the field, each team carrying their banner. These are the little league teams, so you had children from probably kindergarten age to fifth, maybe sixth, grade. The team names were all great, and the little ones who play tee-ball, oh my goodness, they are so cute! After each team was announced, the kids were able to go and play in the park area where they had jump houses, big slides, and carnival-type games. We stayed there until our granddaughter's game began at 1:30 p.m. Her dad is the coach, so of course, we were doubly proud to be there and watch! She is seven, and this is the first season she has played. She is

225

also the catcher! It was a great game, so much fun to watch! We went out to eat afterwards and then went back to the house to visit. Now I will move on to Sunday morning. We woke up early and got ready. We were meeting the kids at the Catholic Church they attend so that we could all go to Mass together. Mass began at 9:00 a.m. Jim and I loved being with our family at Mass! After Mass, the girls showed us where they go to CCD classes. The older one will make her first Holy Communion in May. We are very excited!

Next, we all went to eat breakfast, and then it was time to head back west toward home! We decided to stop in Praha to visit one of the historic Catholic Churches that has been undergoing renovations. St. Mary's Church of the Assumption in Praha, Texas, is a historically beautiful, amazingly designed Catholic Church. The paintings and stained-glass windows, statues, and architectural design will just grab you. This is the second time that Jim and I have been to visit this church. It is listed as one of the painted churches. We arrived about 4:00 p.m., and the doors would not be locked until 5:00 p.m., so we had plenty of time to look at everything. We both knelt down to pray for a little while. Jim walked up to one of the shrines and lit ten candles, one for each of our grandchildren. We walked back outside and went toward the grotto. Jim said he wondered who had given Mother Mary the beautiful flower. I walked into the grotto. The statue of the Assumption of Mother Mary is so beautiful and gives you such a feeling of serenity. I noticed the prettiest dark-red rose lying right in the crook of her arm. I laughed and told Jim that I didn't think he was supposed to pick the flowers. He told me it was just one, the prettiest of them all, and he felt like that was where it belonged. I couldn't argue with that logic! I'll attach the picture of it after I finish this post. We got back into the truck and headed west once more. We were only a few miles down the road when I asked Jim if we could stop and visit Raphael's Refuge in Flatonia, which is only just a little further down the road. I knew he was tired and just wanted to travel on, but I really needed to stop there, and so we did! It had been almost two years since we first found Raphael's Refuge, and I wanted to see how much more work had been done. We thought we might be the only ones out there but were pleasantly surprised to see Midge, the amazing woman who listened to God and donated a large piece of her land for this wonderful place to be built. She was saying good-bye to another woman when we walked up. I said, "Hello, Midge, you probably don't remember us." But you know what? She did. She remembered our first visit and gave us both a big hug. She was so excited to show us around. I will have to share everything about that visit later on.

I will call it "Raphael's Refuge Part 2."

This is their website if you would like to look it up: www. RaphaelsRefuge.org

This is their mission statement: To build and maintain a memorial in honor of babies, born and unborn. To provide peer counseling for those suffering a loss of a baby due to miscarriage, stillbirth, infant death, and abortion.

I'm going to close with this prayer from Raphael's Refuge:

Parent's Prayer for a Departed Baby

Holy Spirit, creator of life and love, thank you
for breathing life into the soul of my baby.
Heavenly Father, thank you for letting me play
a role in my baby's creation.

Lord Jesus, thank you for my baby's love.

From my empty arms, I place my baby into
your arms, to be held for all eternity.

Amen.

The Way I Write
Is the Way I Feel
Words from My Heart

Tuesday, April 19, 2016

Hello out there! We've been blessed with rain! This message I want to share has really been on my heart. I've been trying to find the right words to say, but maybe I just need to jump right in and write the way I feel! Because the truth is, the way I feel is the way I write. Some of my posts are fun and lighthearted, but all my posts come from my heart.

I want to get the message out there that adoption is a life option. I would love to see billboards and commercials and magazine covers of people who have been adopted. I want to hear adoption stories because I know how special each story is! I want people to know that babies are a gift. If you are in a crisis pregnancy and this is not the right time for you to have a baby, please consider adoption for your baby. I was blessed to have been adopted at birth, and I want to share the message that adoption is a life-giving option! I see the commercials on television where the movie stars are holding a puppy or a kitten and they are crying, begging people to adopt these poor innocent animals. That is fine, but what about the poor innocent babies? What about the unborn? Where are the tears? Where is the compassion? Why are people so afraid to speak up for the human babies? If

I had the money to pay for advertising on billboards about adopting the human babies, I would. Maybe I need to get more information about how much it costs and have a fundraiser. Maybe that is why God has placed this on my heart. I write these posts, but I must do more. Thanks for listening. Just writing about this has helped me. It is time for me to take the next step. If you have some ideas, please share them with me. I will keep you posted on the billboard idea. I wrote a post back in September of 2014, and I am going to repost it today because the words I wrote then are how I feel again. God bless you all from wherever you are.

A post from September 2014 (I've tweaked it a little bit. Just following my heart!):

You know, things don't always go as we plan, dream, or hope. Many times, God is reminding us that He is in charge of our lives, not us. Maybe it's a job loss, a transfer, not getting the house you want, or maybe it's something like not having good enough credit for an expensive vehicle or maybe just any kind of vehicle! An unplanned pregnancy definitely changes everything, absolutely changes how you live your life, but if you stop and think about it, this baby is a gift from God. Maybe you need a new direction. This baby will change your life for the better. This baby is part of you. To all the men out there, no matter what age you are, if your girlfriend or wife is pregnant, be a real man. Take care of your family. Take care of your responsibilities. Love, protect, and support them. Be proud to be called Dad. As far as that goes, be proud to be a husband! Take pride in yourself and say, "Hey, it's going to be okay. We can do this." Your girlfriends, your wives, they need to hear you say, "We're a family. Yes, this changes everything, but for the better!" Children need their mothers and their fathers. Babies are such a blessing! When did we get so offtrack? We need commercials and television shows that support family instead of the stupid stuff that's on. We need magazine covers that have positive messages about happy families and not the tabloid trash that is on the rack right by the check-out stand in the stores.

Men, step up to the plate, and be a loving and supportive dad. Be a great boyfriend. Better yet, be a great husband. Make the commitment that says this is for real, this is forever! I realize that the majority of men are wonderful husbands and dads who take great care of their families. I personally know many men who are the ones raising their children. The single dads I know are amazing, and they do a great job taking care of their children.

I am talking about the young men who drive their girlfriends to the abortion facilities and/or those who push them into having an abortion. A baby is not a choice. A baby is a gift, a unique individual and should be loved and cherished. Choosing adoption for your baby if you are not able to raise them is choosing life. I'm not saying that adoption would be an easy decision, but at least you would be giving your baby a chance just like the chance I was given.

I keep seeing all the challenges on Facebook to raise money for good causes, and there is nothing wrong with that. But here is a real challenge: take care of your family. Be there for your family day in and day out. The world tells you that partying is the way to go. Doesn't barhopping get old? What a sad, empty, lonely life. Being part of a loving, caring family is the most amazing gift you can have and give back to others. Put God first. Find a parish home. Get involved. Spend time with your family. Pray with your family. Attend Mass or church with your family. A good marriage is such a blessing, and it is worth all the time and effort. Communication and respect are really important in all relationships.

Ladies, motherhood is the most amazing gift, but be careful who you pick to date and marry. Make sure they want the same things in life that you do. The same goes for men also! Men and women, please make sure that your children, no matter what their age, are protected, loved, and nurtured!

Spend time with them. Turn off all the phones at mealtime. When you are in the car driving them here and there, talk to them, sing with them, laugh with them, and pray with them! Tune out the world, and tune into family.

This ugliness in our world will not change unless we change. We need to get our priorities straight. We need to put God first, family second, and everything else will fall into place. To sum this all up, I'll say it again: a baby is a gift from God. Our lives are gifts from God. What we do with our life and how we treat others, how we love others, is our gift back to God.

So get out there! Reach out and take care of each other. Take care of your family.

Seek, and You Will Find: God Is Always Near!

Thursday, April 21, 2016

Hello out there! How are y'all doing? I am feeling much better today! Tuesday and yesterday, I just felt blah, a case of the sniffles, and blah, blah, blah! Sometimes, I just get so frustrated with what is going on in this crazy old world! Do you ever have days like that? Jim and I went to the noon Mass today, and that was exactly what I needed! I needed to kneel down and pray, listen to the scriptures, and receive Holy Communion! When Mass was over, I knelt down to pray, and I sang very quietly:

"Lead me, Lord. Lead me, Lord, by the light of truth, to seek and to find the narrow way. Be my way. Be my truth. Be my life, my Lord, and lead me, Lord, today!" I smiled at everyone we saw at Mass and stopped to visit with our friends as we were leaving. Jim patiently waited in the vestibule for me, and then out the doors we went! I felt rejuvenated, I felt happy, and I felt at peace! Jim and I talked about how blessed we are to be able to go to Mass during the week also. We don't make it every day, but I'm sure going to try harder to go more often during the week! The next time I read something in the newspaper or on Facebook that gets me down or really makes me angry, I'm going to stop and take time to pray. Sometimes, I need to be reminded about what I need to do when I'm feeling tired, frustrated, and blue!

Ask, and you will receive. Seek, and you will find. Knock, and it will be opened to you. For the one who asks, receives. The one who seeks, finds. The one who knocks, enters. (Matthew 7:7,8)

I hope and pray that your day and rest of the week is blessed with love and joy, with happiness and sunshine, with family and friends! God loves you! He loves all of us so much! Tell Him what is on your mind. He is always listening!

May God bless you all wherever you are! In Jesus's name I pray, amen.

Peace and blessings,
Sharla

Thanking God for Another Day!

Monday, April 25, 2016

Good morning out there! What a beautiful morning! We started our morning bright and early—not really bright because it was still dark outside, but we did start out early! We go to the Adoration Chapel on Monday mornings from 5:00 a.m. to 6:00 a.m. Spending an hour in quiet meditation, prayer, reflection, or reading the daily scriptures is such a great way to start the day. We signed up almost a year and a half ago, and we have really treasured our quiet time of Eucharistic Adoration. I've told y'all before that I am definitely not the early bird in our family, but once I'm up, look out, world. Here I come! On our way home, we stopped and picked up burritos. We walked into the little restaurant at about 6:10 a.m., and there were three ladies working. Jim nodded his head at them and I said, "Good morning. Good morning! Buenos dias!" I was in such a joyful mood I just wanted to spread some happiness. The ladies looked at me kind of shocked and still kind of asleep and mumbled, "Good morning." Jim told me it was way too early for my cheerfulness and that I probably scared them. I just laughed! I was in the best mood, and I had a million things going through my mind. Once we got back in the truck, I started telling Jim all the things I needed to do this week. He said if I didn't calm down, I was going to be so tired by the time we got home I wouldn't be able to get anything done. I just laughed again! I have to share some of the scriptures I read this morning from the *Magnificat*.

"Jesus said to them, 'Go into all the world, and proclaim the Gospel to every creature'" (Mark 16:15).

The response for Psalm 89 is, "Forever I will sing the goodness of the Lord." (I'm singing it.)

Prayer for the morning: "Jesus Christ is the voice of salvation: let us listen and give thanks, alleluia!"

I better get busy if I'm going to accomplish all that I need to do! I hope you all have a wonderful day! Blessings and peace to you and yours!

Bye for now.
Sharla

Love One Another!

Monday, May 2, 2016

Good morning, and hello out there! We are out of regular Folgers Coffee! If you have read very many of my blog posts, you know that this is not a good thing! We do have some decaf, and I drank that, but I will be going out to buy a grande container of my regular coffee today!

I have to go and run errands, like a bazillion of them! Ugh! That is really not something to complain about. I am thankful for a new day! I pray that God will guide me to where I need to be as I run my errands, a smile here and a hug there, maybe a listening ear! Example, Friday night, Jim and I were on our way to watch our oldest grandson play baseball. All of a sudden, I see a man I recognize from the Sack Lunch Ministry, and I whip a U-turn. (Jim says, "Sharla, what are you doing?) I ask Jim to hand me some crackers, a Gatorade, and a bottle of water from the backseat so that I can give it to that man sitting on the park bench. I pulled over and parked, walked over to the man, and said, "Hello, I know you from the Sack Lunch Ministry." He smiled and asked if I wanted to sit down. I explained that I don't have time but I thought he might like something to drink and a snack. He thanked me and waved at my husband. I jumped back in the truck, and we made it to the game just in time! Opportunities are everywhere. Just open your heart to what God is calling you to do!

I just wanted to say hello and that I hope you all have a wonderful, super great blessing-filled day!

Bye for now.

Sharla

Staying on the Right Path!

Saturday, May 7, 2016

Good morning out there! Last night, I opened my *Living Faith* daily Catholic devotions to Friday, May 6. I usually read my devotions in the morning, but I didn't yesterday. The title made my sleepy eyes pop open, "Speaking for Justice." Then I read the scripture: "Do not be afraid. Go on speaking, and do not be silent, for I am with you" (Acts 18:9–10).

I said, "Jim, you will not believe what the daily devotion scriptures for today are!" I felt like the Good Lord was encouraging me to keep on writing, to keep on speaking up for the babies! Yesterday was one of those days where I was really second-guessing myself. God is so good. He knows me so well.

Just the morning before, I woke up at 3:00 a.m. If I wake up during the night, I pray for whatever is really touching my heart. Sometimes, I just say, "Lord, I don't know who needs my prayers right now, but You do, so my prayers are for whoever is in need." The morning I'm telling you about, I knew exactly who I needed to pray for. I just kept seeing babies in my mind, precious little babies. I immediately started praying for all the women who were scheduled to have abortions that day. I prayed that someone would reach out to them and let them know that help is available. I prayed that the fathers of these babies would have an overwhelming sense of love and compassion for their baby and the baby's mother. I prayed that the abortionists would have a change of heart and, if that didn't work, that they would have a flat tire! I prayed for the babies. I prayed that their little lives would be spared. I prayed for a conversion of hearts! I just had to share this with you. Our prayers are needed. Please keep on praying for the unborn, their families, and for families all over the world!

The scripture for this morning from the *Living Faith* daily Catholic devotion is, "Ask and you will receive, so that your joy may be complete" (John 16:24).

Faith Is the Fabric
of Our Lives!

Monday, May 16, 2016

Good morning out there! So much to say, so much to share! Last week was just awesome! Fellowship and fun at the Parish Family Picnic on Wednesday evening! It just warms my heart to see so many families enjoying spending time together: throwing Frisbees, playing football, eating together, laughing, and talking! There were so many families at the picnic, and I loved being part of it!

We traveled out of town on Thursday and headed to the Houston area to visit our oldest son and his family. A very special event was happening on Saturday! We were blessed to see another one of our granddaughters make her first Holy Communion on Saturday. The Mass was wonderful. The homily really hit home. It is so important for parents to be good examples for their children. At home is where the children learn so much about their faith: praying together, going to Mass together, and putting God first in our families. Grandparents, godparents, and Catechists also guide and teach our children. Leading by example was what the homily emphasized. The children were all so reverent when they received Communion, such a beautiful, amazing sacrament. I'm so thankful that we were able to be there. Spending time with our children and grandchildren is always great, and especially when we are celebrating a very happy and joyful occasion! On Sunday, we celebrated Pentecost. The Mass back here at our parish home was a blessing. We were tired from our seven-hour journey back home, but we knew we needed to go to Mass. We unpacked, got ready, and headed to church. We were both so tired but so glad that we made the effort and attended Mass. This morning, we woke up early and went to the Adoration Chapel for our usual Monday morning time. If you read my blog posts on a regular basis, you will understand the following. If you don't, go back and read from two weeks ago, and this will make sense, I think. Guess what? We have real Folgers Coffee in our home now, and I got it ready last night and set the timer! The coffee was ready when we woke up!

Now for the rest of the story!

There were some other really nice things that happened last week, and I feel so very blessed! My cup runneth over! Two weeks ago, I told y'all in one of my blog posts that we had run out of regular Folgers Coffee and we only had decaf. Anyway, that is not a good situation in our household, and I did go out and buy a large container of coffee that very same day. Well, last Monday, I went to help at the Sack Lunch Ministry, and there was a thirty-ounce container of Folgers Coffee sitting on the counter with a note attached to it. It had my name on it, and it said, "To a great lady that needs her cup of Java early in the morning. God bless you and all that you do!" I asked Mrs. Rose who left it for me, and she said it was already there when she arrived. Is that not the neatest thing? I found out later who left it, one of my sweet prayer warriors who comes to pray during the 40 Days for Life Campaigns. I told her that was so thoughtful and she just made my day! Well, on Wednesday, at the family picnic, one of my students gave me a gift. (I teach the fourth grade CCD class.) She wrote the nicest "thank you" note, and inside the cute gift basket was a silver cross that says "Special Teacher," one I can hang on the wall. I'm going to hang it up in my office! There was something else under the tissue paper. It was another container of Folgers Coffee, the breakfast blend kind, and it was a twenty-five-ounce container! I laughed, thanked my sweet student, and looked for her mother. I gave her a hug too, and she replied, "I read your blog!" I told her about the other container of coffee, and we both laughed. That same night, at the picnic, I received another "thank you" note. This note was for both Jim and me. It was from the couple we are helping with their marriage preparation class. The note was thanking us for dinner and for taking the time to help them during this special time in their lives. My heart just grew and grew. I felt so blessed, and I could just feel God's love from each one of these special moments of kindness and friendship. God is so good. I pray that you each receive a special type of blessing in your lives today and the whole week through.

Bye for now.
Sharla

Proud to Be a Pro-Life Chick and a Voice for the Voiceless!

Wednesday, May 18, 2016

Hello out there! I'm listening to the beautiful, soothing sound of rain falling! I hope you all are having a good week. I have been busy catching up on book work and laundry! I made a big pot of spicy chicken and dumplings for lunch today. Jim's working at home right now, so I just hollered out the back door lunch is ready! Apparently, he didn't hear me with the rain beating down on the shop roof and all, so I called him on his cell phone. Isn't that crazy? Calling someone on the phone when they are right outside? Oh well, it worked! We've eaten lunch. He's gone back out to the shop, and I decided to sit down and write for a while.

This morning, I looked through my *Heritage House* catalog. It has all kinds of pro-life items. Everything you might need for display tables, conferences, 40 Days Campaigns, Respect Life Week, etc., you will find in this catalog, or you can shop online. Their website is www.hh76.org.

They carry items like pro-life T-shirts, banners, bumper stickers, bulletin inserts, pamphlets, pins, and more! I would love to order one of all their T-shirts! I think I'm going to order the T-shirt that says, "Pro-Life Chick," and it has a baby chick on it! Another one of my favorites says, "I Am a Voice for the Voiceless." All the T-shirts have really great messages on them.

Today, I was looking for a particular item. Fetal Models: The Touch of Life Set. The description on the box says, "Soft, life-like and exquisite detail," and has information about the gestation of a baby from conception to birth. There are four fetal models—a baby at twelve weeks (14 LMP), sixteen weeks (18 LMP), twenty-two weeks (24 LMP), and twenty-six weeks (28 LMP). I have a set of these fetal models, and I set them up on my display table along with pamphlets during the 40 Days for Life Campaign kick-off rallies and at other pro-life talks I have given.

The children are really drawn to these life-like babies. Teenagers are always amazed at how they look just like a baby even when they are very small. Each fetal model looks like how a baby would look at that stage of development. I ordered two sets today. Jim and I are donating a set to the Pro-Life Rams, a pro-life group of students from Angelo State University, and the other set is for Raiders Defending Life, a pro-life group of students from Texas Tech University. I went to a pro-life conference that the Pro-Life Rams sponsored about a month ago, and I noticed that they had the small set of fetal models, seven weeks to ten weeks, out on display. I told them about the display set I had and asked them if they would like to have a set of the twelve weeks to twenty-six weeks, and they said yes! About ten students representing Raiders Defending Life were at the conference also. The president of the group is from here, and I asked her if they would like a set. These pro-life students work really hard to defend life, and I am thankful that we are able to provide these fetal model displays for them to use at their events! Jim says I have to wait and order the T-shirts later, and that's okay. I think everyone knows that I'm a pro-life chick and that I try really hard to be a voice for the voiceless! That makes me think of something else that is kind of funny.

When Jim and I were out of town last weekend, I said something about how our white truck is incognito because there are so many white trucks. Jim replied that it is kind of hard to be incognito when you have "In God We Trust" in black on the tail gate, a bumper sticker that says "40 Days for Life—Pray to End Abortion," and a 91.5 Catholic Radio Station bumper sticker on the rear of the white truck! I started laughing hard because what he said was so true! I thought, "Oh my goodness, I'm talking even when I'm not talking, and that is okay because that's just me!" I hope y'all have a great day!

Go out and be a voice for the voiceless! Pray to end abortion! Hug your kids, hug your spouse, and thank God. Thank Him, and thank Him, and thank Him!

Bye for now.
Sharla

Family and Friends and a Little Quiet Time!

Sunday, May 22, 2016

Hello out there! It is a quiet and peaceful Sunday afternoon at the Ynostrosa Hacienda. Last week, our home was the center of activity. Monday evening, we had four of our grandchildren with us. I had a large rump roast with veggies cooking in the oven and a pot of beans soaking. The older kids played outside, and the younger ones stayed inside. Jim was out in the shop trying to finish up a project. I fed them and bathed them, and then their dad arrived. He was just finishing up a job; he had to work late, and his wife was at a Catholic Daughter's meeting. After he ate, we loaded up the kids and waved good-bye. Jim finally finished the project and came inside. It was 9:00 p.m. by the time we sat down to eat. Our home was quiet once more.

Tuesday morning, I picked up one of my dearest friends, and we headed to San Antonio for her doctor's appointment. We talked all the way there, catching up and sharing news about our children and grandchildren. After her appointment,, we stopped to eat a late lunch and then headed back to San Angelo. The clouds were dark, and it rained on and off. We both received calls from our family telling us to be careful, that bad weather was headed our way. We prayed the Divine Mercy Chaplet and arrived safely home without any problems.

Wednesday morning, my daughter and youngest granddaughter stopped by for a visit. She brought her dad some chocolate-chip cookie bars. She had made a large batch. Jim loves cookies! I filled a large bowl with red beans, the ones I had cooked on Monday night, and sent that with her. They love fresh-cooked red beans! Thursday morning, my daughter and youngest granddaughter came back over to help me clean house! Jim and I were expecting company for the weekend, so Jess and I tag-teamed the housework: stripping beds, washing sheets, cleaning bathrooms, etc. Friday morning, I went to the grocery store at 7:30 a.m. and bought groceries for the weekend. It was great. There was hardly anybody there that early! I bought a small bouquet of yellow tulips and put them in a vase when I got home. I put away the groceries, and then I took care of two of my granddaughters while my daughter went to the beauty shop. Friday afternoon, our friends from out of town arrived. They had only been here about fifteen minutes when a friend of ours from church stopped by. He stayed and visited with us for a little while and then went on his way. Our son and his family stopped by to visit before our oldest grandson's baseball game. We have been friends with this couple for years, lots of years! They are more like family: godparents to two of our children, he was best man at our wedding, my husband is their son's godfather (I wasn't in the picture yet), and she took me under her wing when Jim and I got married! They moved away years ago, but we have always stayed close. They were in town for a graduation and were going to spend the night at our home. We went to our grandson's baseball game, and they went to the graduation. When they got back, we decided that since it was such a nice evening (10:30 p.m.), we would sit out on the back porch. We sat out there, a citronella candle burning, the radio playing oldies, a glass of wine for us, a beer for them, and we talked and laughed, and we talked and laughed some more! At 1:30 a.m., we came back inside and called it a night. I made the coffee, set the timer, and went to bed. At 8:30 a.m., Jim told me to get up because everyone was awake. I frowned at him, but I did get up. We had a cup of coffee, and then we loaded up in their truck and went out to eat breakfast. On the way home, we stopped by our daughter and son-in-law's home so that they could visit for a few minutes. After we got back here, they packed. We made plans to get together again soon and waved good-bye.

Then Jim and I got back into the truck and went to pick up our grandsons because they were going to spend the day with us. The rest of the day were haircuts, birthday party at the bowling alley, helping Pa outside, dinner, showers, Despicable Me 2, hugs, and lights out (it ended up being a sleepover). A very, very tired Nana and Pa went to bed.

This morning, we woke up and literally dragged ourselves out of bed. Jim fixed the boys something to eat, and then we headed toward their home (about forty-five minutes away). We usually meet in the middle, but I was moving slow, and so our son had to drive a little farther this time. Hugs, good-byes, and off we drove, separate directions, back to our homes.

Jim and I quietly read the newspaper and then tidied up.

It is quiet right now, but it won't last long!

I hope you all have a restful Sunday, a little time to recharge your batteries.

I'm going to rest for a few minutes before I get ready for the 6:00 p.m. Mass. God bless you all.

Bye for now.

Sharla

Cookies, Beer Bread, and Thirty-Three Years of Marriage: It's All Good!

Thursday, June 2, 2016

    Hello out there! I haven't posted in almost a week! How are y'all doing? It has been raining on and off all week. Right now, it is overcast and a little cool outside, 70 degrees to be exact. For this time of year, 70 degrees is awesome! The only thing negative about this kind of weather is it makes me want to bake! I saw some chocolate chips in the pantry, and so I decided to check and see what other ingredients I have on hand. I have everything I need to make a big batch of chocolate-chip oatmeal cookies with pecans! Doesn't that sound great? I also have the ingredients to make beer bread. I haven't made beer bread since the Christmas season because I sure don't need to eat it, but it sounds really good today! *And* it is so easy to make! I will share the recipe with y'all! Easy peasy and only four ingredients!

    To 3 1/2 cups self-rising flour, add 1/2 cup sugar and stir together. Add 1 can (12 oz.) of room-temperature beer (I use Lone Star because that is what Jim drinks and so I have it on hand). Stir until well-blended, batter will be kind of lumpy. Spoon into a greased (I use the Crisco spray stuff) loaf/bread pan. My loaf pans are glass, but the aluminum/metal pans work just as well. Bake in a preheated 350 degree oven for fifty minutes. This bread smells so good when it is baking! Melt 1/2 stick of butter (the recipe calls for 1 stick, but 1/2 is a little less fattening!). Melt the butter and pour it all over the top of the bread, and then put the bread back into the oven for another ten minutes. Wait as long as you can, and then slice and enjoy! Add more butter if you want, but it really doesn't need it. This bread is great with soups, stews, or a big pot of red beans and as toast! I haven't tried it as garlic bread, but I bet that it would be great that way too! There is also a really good biscuit recipe on the back of the self-rising flour. This reminds me of another baking tip to pass along. If you want to make buttermilk biscuits and don't have or keep buttermilk on hand, this tip will work.

Use 1 teaspoon of vinegar for each 1/3 cup of milk. If your recipe calls for 1 cup of buttermilk, add 3 teaspoons or 1 tablespoon of vinegar to your milk, and let it sit for at least five minutes. I usually add the vinegar to the milk first thing, and then by the time I get to that step, it has already been plenty of time for the milk to sour. I really had not planned on writing about recipes or cooking tips today, but sometimes, that is what happens!

On Saturday, Jim and I will be married for thirty-three years! I can't believe it! The years have flown by. I thank God every day for blessing me with such a wonderful husband. One of my favorite scriptures from the Bible is from Genesis, when Adam sees Eve for the first time.

> So the Lord God cast a deep sleep on the man, and while he was asleep, he took out one of his ribs and closed up its place with flesh. The Lord God then built up into a woman the rib that he had taken from the man. When he brought her to the man, the man said:

> "This one, at last, is bone of my bones and flesh of my flesh; This one shall be called 'woman,' for out of 'her man' this one has been taken." That is why a man leaves his father and mother and clings to his wife, and the two of them become one body. (Genesis 2:21–24)

Another one of my favorite scriptures that I think is so important for a happy marriage and a loving family is this one:

> Love is patient; love is kind. Love is not jealous, it does not put on airs, it is not snobbish. Love is never rude, it is not self-seeking, it is not prone to anger; neither does it brood over injuries. Love does not rejoice in what is wrong but rejoices with the truth. There is no limit to love's forbearance, to its trust, its hope, its power to endure. (1 Corinthians 13:4–7)

I hope you all have a wonderful day. If you try the beer bread recipe, let me know if you like it. I hope the vinegar substitution helps also! God bless you all!

Bye for now.
Sharla

Walking and Praying: Spending Some Quiet Time with God!

Tuesday, June 7, 2016

Hello out there! The sun is shining, and the flowers are blooming, and the birds are flying everywhere! Yesterday, Jim and I watched a little humming bird getting pollen from some flowers in one of our hanging baskets. Their wings flutter so fast as they move from flower bud to flower bud. We have a large window right in front of our kitchen table. There is a small window right above the kitchen sink. Both of these windows face our front yard. We love watching the birds and the squirrels! These windows are on the west side of our home, and we are able to look out and see all the beautiful sunsets. The colors of the sky have been so many different hues of pink, orange, and blue the last week or so. The clouds have also been neat to watch, so many varying shapes and colors. This morning, I went for a walk on a road that is close to the lake, about two miles long and has a natural incline. Many people walk, run, and bike on this very popular road. I saw lizards darting across the road, colorful butterflies, and all kinds of birds as I walked. It was about 76 degrees outside and not windy at all. I walked and prayed and enjoyed being outside on such a beautiful morning. I felt so at peace when I got back to my truck. I ran some errands, took lunch to my husband, and took care of some invoices for our family business.

I don't have anything major to tell y'all about or any crazy stories to share. I just wanted to check in and say hi. I hope you all have a really great day. Take time to watch the sun set and the birds fly.

Take a few minutes, and just be with God. You will be so glad you did! Peace be with you and your family!

> The eyes of the Lord are upon those who love him; He is their mighty shield and strong support. A shelter from the heat, a shade from the noonday sun, a guard against stumbling, a help against falling. He buoys up the spirits, brings a sparkle to the eyes, gives health and life and blessing. (Sirach 34:16,17)

> O Lord, my rock, my fortress, my deliverer. My God, my rock of refuge, my shield, the horn of my salvation, my stronghold! (Psalm 18:3)

Bye for now.
Sharla

Sunshine, Sack Lunches and Corporal Works of Mercy

Tuesday, June 14, 2016

Hello out there! It is a little after 7:00 p.m. and 93 degrees! I was outside filling up my bird bath and spritzing my plants! I decided it was still too hot and came inside. Jim is still out there. He was busy feeding all the animals and refilling all the water containers. I take care of keeping our dog's and cat's water bowls full, and Jim takes care of the sheep and chickens. One of my ferns is growing really large and is starting to hide my statue of Mother Mary. That fern will be cut back tomorrow, early in the morning! My morning glories and passion vines are spreading all over the place. All the plants look so pretty. We have been blessed with so much rain the past month, and the grass, weeds, trees, and flowers love it!

I helped at the Sack Lunch Ministry today. They already had all the lunches ready when I got there, so I started coloring! I grabbed a bunch of sacks and wrote messages on them and drew flowers. I keep it simple. I write things like, "You Are Special! God Loves You! Jesus Loves You! God Is Good!" After I had been there for a while, my daughter dropped off two of my granddaughters to help. They love to visit with everyone and help out. They sat down and began coloring too! The oldest one draws really well. She wrote her own messages, "Be Merciful! Be kind to one another! Be thankful! Take care of each other!" Sometimes, I learn as much from them as they learn from me. There was plenty of help, so we decided to go to the noon Mass, also known as the worker's Mass. It starts at 12:10 p.m. and only lasts about thirty minutes. After Mass, we went to pick up chicken feed, and then I took the girls home.

Tomorrow, I have to work on filing, writing out invoices, paying bills, and organizing my home office. I get busy doing other things and helping out, and before you know it, Jim is asking if he needs to hire a secretary? I always laugh and tell him that I will get it done! I do have to get up early and go buy supplies for the Sack Lunches, deliver them, and *then* I will get started on my bookwork!

I hope you all have a great week! I will write another post soon! I am going to close with the Corporal Works of Mercy.

> To feed the hungry.
> To give drink to the thirsty.
> To clothe the naked.
> To welcome the stranger.
> To heal the sick.
> To visit the imprisoned.
> To bury the dead.

At the Sack Lunch Ministry, we feed the hungry, give drink to the thirsty, and welcome the stranger five days a week! During the winter months, we hand out gloves and warm jackets, sweaters, and coats. Some people donated shoes, socks, and boots! Warm caps, hats, and some brand-new sleeping bags were donated too! I heard that someone dropped off some backpacks for us to hand out tomorrow! I love being part of this much-needed ministry! I think I will buy some Gatorade to hand out with the water because the next couple of days are going to be really hot! I was thinking about what my granddaughter wrote, "Take care of each other!" Yes, Gatorades will be needed this week!

Blessings to you and yours!

Bye for now.
Sharla

July 4, 2016 – Ten Grandchildren - Bountiful Blessings

My Prayer for You

I pray that your day is full of blessings.

If you are sick, I pray that you will get well.

If you have lost a loved one, I pray that you will be comforted.

If you are anxious, I pray that a feeling of peace will wash over you.

If you are lonely, I pray that someone will reach out to you.

I pray that you will know that even though I may not know you, I really do care.

If you are struggling financially, I pray that God will send you what you need.

If you are struggling with addiction, I pray that God will give you strength

And courage to give up whatever is holding you hostage.

If you are in a crisis pregnancy, I pray that you will be directed to the path of life,

And guided to all the help that is available for you and your baby.

If you are a caregiver, I pray that you will get the rest you need,

And know that it is okay to take time for yourself.

Dear God, I pray for peace all across the whole world.

I pray for peace in every country. I pray for those who seek refuge.

I pray for those who are hungry and thirsty. I pray for the homeless and the lonely.

I lift all the intentions I've listed above to You, God our Father.

I pray for anyone and everyone who might be suffering or going through

Any of the things I've written about.

Please God, show us how to take care of each other, to love one another,

And help us to be discerning in all that we do. Thank you for today, please guide us,

And help us to live the way you want us to. Please keep us safe and help us to look to You,

And not the world for direction and answers.

In Jesus's name I pray, Amen.

Notes

1. The following hymns are mentioned throughout my stories. I've included either the refrain and/or a verse from the hymns: "Blest are They" – Composer: David Haas – GIA Publications, Inc. "Lead me, Lord" – Composer: John D. Becker – Published by OCP "They'll Know We are Christians" – Author: Peter Scholtes (1938-2009) F.E.L. Publications, assigned to The Lorenz Corp., 1991 "We are Called" – Composer: David Haas – GIA Publications, Inc. "We are Many Parts" – Composer: Marty Haugen – GIA Publications, Inc.

2. The scriptures included in the stories with the following dates are from the - Saint Joseph Edition of the New American Bible: Thursday, April 24, 2014; Saturday, May 3, 2014; Tuesday, January 6, 2015; Friday, January 30, 2015; Friday, June 12, 2015; Friday, June 26, 2015; Thursday, April 21, 2016; Thursday, June 2, 2016; Tuesday, June 7, 2016

3. The scriptures that are included with the rosary on Tuesday, July 15, 2014 and Thursday, April 30, 2015 are from the pamphlet, "Pray the Rosary Daily" published by Marian Press

4. The scripture from the story for Tuesday, May 27, 2014 is from the book, "Together for Life" written by Joseph M. Champlin – Ave Maria Press

5. The scripture from the story for Thursday, March 27, 2014 is from a brochure from – Gladney Center for Adoption

6. Many scriptures are from the – "Living Faith Daily Catholic Devotions" or the "Magnificat" and are listed in the story when referenced

7. The remaining scriptures are from various sources; daily desk calendars, brochures, etc. – NIV or NRSV follow these scriptures

8. I am the author of the poem on the first page, the prayer on the last page, and some of the poems and prayers throughout my stories.

About the Author

Sharla Ynostrosa is a devoted wife, mother, and grandmother. Her ten grandchildren keep her busy! She and her husband, Jim, have been married thirty-three years and are the owners of JY Welding. Sharla's family is her top priority. Reading stories to her grandchildren and baking for them are some of her favorite activities. She also enjoys planting flowers and watching the birds, squirrels, peacocks, and chickens that visit her front yard. Having been adopted at birth, Sharla is a staunch pro-life advocate. She has a pro-life blog www. adoptedandblessed.blogspot.com and has submitted several articles to her local newspaper about pro-life issues. She and her husband live in San Angelo, Texas, and are active members in their parish, Sacred Heart Cathedral.

This refrain is from one of her favorite hymns and is her constant prayer: "Lead me, Lord. Lead me, Lord, by the light of truth, to seek and to find the narrow way. Be my way. Be my truth. Be my life, my Lord, and lead me, Lord, today."

CPSIA information can be obtained
at www.ICGtesting.com
Printed in the USA
BVOW05*0729290517

485401BV00014B/152/P